Reclaiming Your Future

♦ ♦ ♦

There is only one thing harder than a Twelve-Step program, and that is getting beyond it.

From this book, you will learn:

- How to design a personal relapse prevention program
- How to recognize seven warning signs of stress
- The hidden losses that may be sabotaging your life
- Why reliving a childhood crisis may be the most crucial step in moving beyond recovery
- Why your deepest feelings can work against you and how you can make them your allies

Kendall Johnson, Ph.D., has done pioneering work in the areas of trauma and stress management. His recent work, *Turning Yourself Around: Self-Help Strategies for Troubled Teens* is considered one of the freshest, most dynamic books in the field of dependency and recovery. Now he has put together a guide that will take you through recovery and beyond, to new horizons of personal growth and transformation.

FELLOWSHIP SOUVENIRS
& RECOVERY ENTERPRISES
PENWITH BUSINESS CENTRE
LONG ROCK
PENZANCE, CORNWALL. TR20 8HL
Tel: 01736 332205 Fax: 01736 352017
E.MAIL:
FELLOWSHIPSOUVENIRS@YAHOO.COM

Other books by Kendall Johnson

Trauma in the Lives of Children
Turning Yourself Around
School Crisis Management

No More Hurt
Living with My Family
(With Wendy Deaton)

Growth and Recovery Workbook Series
(Consulting editor)

RECLAIMING YOUR FUTURE

Finding Your Path After Recovery

Kendall Johnson, Ph.D.

Hunter House

Copyright © 1993 by Kendall Johnson, Ph.D.

All rights reserved. No part of this publication may be reproduced or transmitted in any form or by any means, electronic or mechanical, including photocopying, recording, or introduced into any information storage and retrieval system without the written permission of the copyright owner and the publisher of this book. Brief quotations may be used in reviews prepared for inclusion in a magazine, newspaper, or broadcast. For further information contact:

Hunter House Inc., Publishers
P.O. Box 2914
Alameda, CA 94501-0914

Library of Congress Cataloging-in-Publication Data
Johnson, Kendall
Reclaiming your future : Finding your path after recovery / Kendall Johnson.
p. cm.
ISBN 0-89793-093-2 : $10.95
1. Twelve-step programs. 2. Compulsive behavior—Relapse—Prevention. 3. Substance abuse—Relapse—Prevention. I. Title.
RC533.K45 1992
158".1—dc20 92-38002

Cover design by Beth Hansen
Book design by Qalagraphia
Editors: Gina Gross, Lisa E. Lee, Kiran Rana
Production manager: Paul J. Frindt
Publisher: Kiran S. Rana
Typeset by 847 Communications, Alameda CA
Printed by Griffin Printing, Sacramento, CA
Manufactured in the United States of America

9 8 7 6 5 4 3 2 1   First edition

Acknowledgements

Contrary to what you may have read elsewhere, books are not written by authors, they are written by the totality of an author's learning experiences. In this sense books are written by the world as it finds its way through the author.

In another, more immediate sense, books are written by a team consisting of the author, publisher, editor, designer, production manager, marketing specialist, and every other person who contributes to the final product. It has been my very good fortune to have been included as author on the book production team at Hunter House. Paul Frindt, Lisa Lee, Scott Coatsworth, Robin Donovan, Corrie Sahli, and editorial consultant Gina Gross helped write this book, and to them I am grateful.

A personal note of thanks is due to publisher Kiran Rana. My relationship to Kiran over the past few years has been special to me. Kiran has pushed me and always believed that I could rise to the challenges he presented. Obviously this book would not have taken the present form without the Hunter House team, their expertise and their integrity. But in an important way the project would never have been written without Kiran himself. At a critical moment, Kiran challenged me to write beyond myself. I was given the opportunity to synthesize concepts and directions toward which I had been heading in my clinical work and my own life for several years. To meet that challenge was a stretch for me. Kiran, thank you for the faith, encouragement, and motivation you so skillfully wield.

Dedication

Some books insist upon being written. It's too bad they can't write themselves, because birthing books sometimes puts unholy strain upon the bonds of matrimony. This was a hard one at our home. For her patience and tenacious commitment which were tested far beyond reason, this book is appreciatively dedicated to Wendy Christine Losh who (surprisingly) remains my wife.

Table of Contents

	Introduction	1
Part I	Getting Through Recovery	7
1.	Twelve-Step Language and Spirituality	10
2.	"Know Thyself..."	30
3.	Making Amends and Meaning It	46
4.	Managing Stress, Preventing a Relapse	59
Part II	Healing the Past Within Us	80
5.	Letting Go of Past Hurt	83
6.	Working with Loss and Grief	108
7.	Taking Care of Family Business	128
Part III	Reclaiming the Future	153
8.	Your Original Life Trajectory	155
9.	A Pilgrim's Progress	169
	Afterword	190
	Resources	193

Important Notice

The material in this book is intended to provide a guide for dealing with problem behavior and addiction. Any exercises described should be undertaken with the guidance or under the supervision of a licensed therapist or Twelve-Step practitioner. The publisher, author, and editors cannot be held responsible for any errors or omissions. The author and publisher assume no responsibility for any outcome of the use of these materials in self-care programs or in use by a professional.

If you have any questions or concerns about the use or appropriateness of any materials in this book, we strongly recommend that you consult a licensed therapist.

The persons and events described in the vignettes in this book are fictitious. Any resemblance to persons living or dead is purely coincidental.

Introduction

The crowd of Vietnam veterans, Air Force personnel, their families, and a scattering of onlookers waited expectantly. The touring model of the Washington Vietnam Memorial "Wall" had stopped at Norton Air Force Base in California, and was being dedicated. Retired USAF Major Sherry Hoyt stepped up to the microphone. It was seventeen years since her demobilization as flight nurse following two tours in Vietnam, and two years since she began her new civilian role as base benefits director for service families.

In her invocation Sherry made a special plea to those members of the audience who were veterans, and who were still suffering from their participation in that war:

> Four years ago I didn't know what Post-traumatic Stress Disorder was, let alone think I had it. My world was personally and professionally falling apart, but I thought I was fine. While I was at a conference in San Diego I heard a presentation by now retired Admiral James Sears. It was titled "The Wounded Healer." He opened with a story about a nurse who went to the war zone when she was thirty-four. Her fellow nurses were inexperienced, many disliked her—there was great turmoil and no support. Admissions were staggering and in a seventeen-day period there were four thousand casualties. She estimated that one winter she witnessed two thousand deaths. She was known to spend many hours on her knees dressing wounds. She was miserably de-

pressed and obsessed by fear of failure. At one point she wrote, "I am in a state of chronic rage. I saw men hopeless, speechless, dying like Greeks as they wrapped their heads in blankets and never said a word."

She served in the war zone for nearly two years. On her return, she refused an official reception and walked home alone. She was in a state of mental turmoil. She cried, she prayed, she paced endlessly. She couldn't sleep, and when she dozed she had dreams of mutilation. She was exhausted, angry, and depressed. She suffered from shortness of breath and palpitations and was told she must go to bed and rest. She longed for death and was obsessed with feelings of guilt, failure, and death. She lived her life as an invalid until her death fifty-three years later. Her name was Florence Nightingale.

I was shocked. All I had ever heard about her was her courage, her dedication to duty, her love of her country, and her contributions to military and civilian nursing. She was my John Wayne, my idol. That day she became real, and for the first time in fifteen years, I cried—for her, her war, her pain, her men—for me, my war, my pain, and my men.

In a sense, Sherry Hoyt is a pilgrim. She had originally been drawn to nursing to follow an ideal: that of her role model, Florence Nightingale. She had shown promise and advanced in the service. This achievement did not, however, translate into personal serenity and satisfaction. Sherry's pilgrimage was interrupted in the same way as that of her idol—an extended immersion into the horror of war.

> We received up to three hundred casualties a day.... I saw and smelled the napalm burns, infected wounds,

and amputated limbs. I controlled my nausea and held back my tears. I was taught that nurses do not cry or tell their patients how serious or senseless the situation is.... I would not, could not think of these men as my brother, father, uncle, friend, or lover, as I did not know how to deal with the waste, suffering, and wounded bodies.

When I became a flight nurse in 1970 and flew C-141 missions, I shut off more feelings—those of fear, hopelessness, and anger.

Sherry served two tours, caring for the broken and dying. And she emerged from that experience much as Florence Nightingale did, decorated, applauded, and deeply scarred. Unlike her idol, and despite the post-traumatic repercussions of her Vietnam experience, Sherry's work in the military continued beyond the field. Her personal life suffered, however, manifesting in painful symptoms:

I blocked the memories and emotionally stuffed how I felt. I overate, drank, spent money recklessly, traveled the world, had numerous superficial affairs, and became an arrogant, angry workaholic.

This inner battle raged for fifteen years.

When I turned forty, the Challenger shuttle exploded, the B-2 crashed, I was passed over for Lieutenant Colonel for the third time, and my war-hero fighter-pilot husband said he couldn't live with me any longer. I contemplated suicide and ended up in the mental health clinic—flashbacks, nightmares, guilt, shame, anger, death, dying, losses, body bags, IVs going dry, blood-soaked dressings. I needed help—the tough nurse broke. I was now the casualty, lost, alone, frightened, in pain, and crying in the dark....

Sherry Hoyt's is a dramatic, but not uncommon, story. She exemplifies a great many people who have suffered terribly, and as a result of their suffering, live lives of dependency and despair. But Sherry found a way to turn her life around. I met her when she began to reconnect with her original inspirations and ambitions.

Sherry had experienced a derailment from her original life trajectory which took her far afield from the fulfillment her talents and efforts once promised. The mire of post-traumatic reactions, the chaos of dependency, had left her living a life of pain and frustration. Needing to find her way back, several years ago Sherry Hoyt set out on her personal road to recovery. With the help of friends, a counselor, other veterans, participation in a Twelve-Step program, courage, and persistence, Sherry stabilized her life.

Faced with a dependency or addiction that overwhelms their lives, few people are able to look beyond recovery. As she progressed in her recovery, however, Sherry was not satisfied with stabilization. Like many people who pass successfully through Twelve-Step programs and find some stability and a personal equation with their daily needs, she asked, What's next? Like many people, she wanted to believe that the struggle was over. But recovery is a beginning, not an end.

Recovery is recovery from fragmentation, division, and it is the start of a healing process, the other end of which is wholeness. Despite the success stories of thousands, even millions of people in Twelve-Step programs, recovery is still a very fragile process. The first part of this book gives some ideas for dealing with particular issues or stumbling blocks which make recovery especially difficult.

For many of us the dependencies from which we suffer have their basis in earlier traumas such as victimization, social violence, overwhelming loss, or twisted family relationships. While we are still in recovery, we begin to glimpse these underlying issues that need a deeper, more specific type of work. Until we can address and resolve them, we will continue to battle with our dependency—in a sense the dependency is a symptom of the deeper disease.

We have to return to the trauma, loss, or abuse that derailed us and deal with it, on our own or in therapy. So the second part of this book deals with three major life traps: unresolved past hurt, the hidden sabotage of unrecognized loss, and the pain of unfinished family business. The demons that lurk in the dark have to be brought to light so we can sense their deeper message and see their potential as allies.

Having stabilized the present and faced our past, we are prepared for a great evolution. We are truly ready to move beyond recovery and into our future. This third phase can be likened to learning to fly again. We learn to reopen ourselves to the creative, vital, original voice within us that was hidden or suppressed by terror and pain. We may simply redefine our tasks and priorities, and make gradual changes in our lives which bring more personal fulfillment, a greater sense of self-worth, fuller harmony between our inner needs and our outer actions. Or we may choose a grand gesture, a "new" beginning. Either way, we connect with the original life path we started on in all simplicity and trust years before, as children. And then we can reclaim the one thing we truly own, that is truly ours: we can reclaim our ever-manifesting potential, our becoming, our future.

In her work as a benefits counselor, Sherry Hoyt found her peace by reconnecting with her original calling to aid those in pain in a wider, more far-reaching way. Gradually, she was able to move past trauma, past recovery. Now, her life is re-opening to its new trajectory. As she transforms her experience and suffering into new tools for self-fulfillment, Sherry Hoyt is reclaiming her future. She is following the path this book describes.

Part I

Getting Through Recovery

Twelve steps to freedom: that is the promise of Alcoholics Anonymous programs. The Twelve Steps were designed by two alcoholics who worked together to overcome their addiction and regain control over their lives. They recorded the steps they had followed during the course of their recovery and created group programs based on them.

These twelve steps work. Over the years since AA was formed, the Twelve Steps have brought sobriety, recovery, and serenity to millions of alcoholics worldwide. These steps represent an inherently therapeutic approach to dealing with problems and have been used by other groups in dealing with other addictive and compulsive behaviors.

Compulsive and addictive behaviors rob us of our future, strip energy and resources from us, make difficult situations worse, alienate us from those who love us, and leave chaos in their wake. The first step toward reclaiming our future is stabilizing that chaos this book presentes new strategies for stabilization.

Getting into recovery and getting through recovery are two different things. We can become abstinent but still be in misery, continually buffeted by our impulses and needs. We may even find ourselves substituting the recovery lifestyle for our addiction. We compulsively run between meetings, self-help books, and exclusive circles of recovery friends, unable to break a dependency on the recovery program itself. This can be the result of both unfinished work within ourselves and problems in the "program" of recovery.

Many writers and speakers have provided wonderful ideas and insights in recovery books in the last decade, enhancing the success of these programs. Four problem areas, however, make it difficult to fully enter into and adequately work through a program. Unresolved, these issues prevent closure.

The first stumbling block is the language of the Steps themselves. For many, the Steps are written in a style which is not only outdated but unsuited for success. The religious tone of those Steps which speak of a God or Higher Power suggest a limited, exclusive, and dogmatic form of spirituality. Many people find themselves trying to work the Steps while glossing over the spiritual element, thereby undercutting a rich and central resource for themselves.

A second level of problems arises in the personal inventory phase. Though the peer-group setting of Twelve-Step programs is clearly one of their great strengths, often there is inadequate space for the individual feedback and insight that skilled therapy and other forms of self-analysis provide.

Thirdly, circumstances often conspire to make amend-making difficult, counterproductive, or even impossible. Death, separation, or situations where amend-making would hurt other people involved can stymie the amend-making process. Yet, amend-making is central to the therapeutic value of the program.

Finally, though the last three, relapse maintenance Steps are crucial, they give inadequate guidance for managing the main factor in relapse: stress. In order to be effective, a relapse prevention plan must be based in a stress management program.

The first part of this book, then, addresses these weaknesses in the Twelve Step program directly and provides strategies for dealing with them. In these chapters I propose a contemporary revision of the steps and explore a more inclusive spirituality; give some basic techniques for realistic self-assessment; provide creative approaches to amend-making; and outline a stress management model of relapse prevention. Use Part I as the necessary first step to enhance recovery program work and restabilize the present. Parts II and III go on to address the factors which underlie our dysfunctional behavior and discuss ways to move beyond them—and our recovery from them.

1

Twelve-Step Language and Spirituality

Language shapes our perceptions, our thinking, and our possibilities. The more restrictions or assumptions we include or accept in our language, the fewer options we have. When we attempt to follow a program that was designed for someone else or some other time, we may, for a while, be able to accept ideas that don't fit with our own. After a while, though, this goes against our grain and places artificial stumbling blocks along our path to recovery.

The Twelve Steps: A New Look...

If we are struggling with early stages of recovery, we should examine the language of the Twelve Steps and rethink their meaning and our progress. Written in the 1930s, the Steps reflect a culture which nowadays seems exclusive. The spiritual language of the Steps seems to require a certain theology, including a male image of God. The Steps appear to be useful for alcoholics only. Finally, because the Steps were written originally as a report, they read awkwardly. Thus many people are so put off by the original language, they cannot relate to the very process that could save them.

For these reasons I always use an adapted version of the Twelve Steps. These directly follow the spirit of the original program, but use language which is:

- problem neutral, and easily applied to problems other than alcohol
- theologically neutral, and fits a wide variety of spiritual orientations
- gender equal, and does not claim that God is male
- personalized, focusing on the individual

The revised steps that I use read as follows:

1. Admit your powerlessness over your problem and your inability to manage your life.
2. Come to believe that a power greater than you can restore you to strength.
3. Make a decision to turn your will and life over to the care of your Higher Power.
4. Make a searching and honest moral inventory of yourself.
5. Admit to your Higher Power, yourself, and to another human being the exact nature of your wrongs.
6. Prepare to have your Higher Power remove all of your limitations.

7. Humbly ask your Higher Power to remove all of your limitations.
8. Make a list of all the persons you have harmed, and become willing to make amends to them all.
9. Make direct amends to these people wherever possible, except when it would hurt them or others.
10. Continue to make a personal inventory and when you are wrong admit it promptly.
11. Use prayer and meditation to improve your conscious contact with your Higher Power, trying to understand that Power's will and asking for the power to carry that out.
12. Try to use the insights you have gained through your spiritual awakening to carry this message to others who are in trouble.

Recognizing a Higher Power

It takes a great deal to admit our powerlessness over alcohol, drugs, food, relationships, or other compulsions or addictions. The more insecure we are, the more important control is to us. We can suffer for years, denying our suffering and blaming it upon others. Holding on to delusions of control seems like a source of strength and pride. But pride has always been a double-edged sword and control is no source of strength. Control that keeps a deteriorating situation in place is called denial, and denial of weakness robs us of energy and options. Denial keeps us from understanding just what we are up against. Military victories, for example, are never won by underestimating an enemy's strength or ignoring their tactics. They are won by strategically utilizing all one's resources.

There is a story of a wise father who, while walking through the garden, came upon his son who was straining mightily to lift a very large rock. Not wishing to usurp his son's efforts, the father asked, "Son, are you using all of your strength?"

"Yes, Father," replied the boy through clenched teeth, his veins standing out on his neck.

"No, my son, you are not," the father said. "You haven't asked me to help you."

The point of this story is not that God is a benevolent father or savior. It is that we often struggle blindly against obstacles larger than ourselves. Until we develop the self-awareness, humility, and grace to call upon all of the powers available to us, we will continue to experience defeat.

While many people worry that Step Two—believing that a power greater than you can restore you to strength—suggests that traditional religious beliefs are a prerequisite for recovery, this is not the case. Step Two simply acknowledges that surrendering false control is a powerful resource available to all, a personal process rather than a dogma.

Your addiction or compulsion made you act irrationally and against your own interests. Your pride and belief that you could handle anything resulted in your losing control. Now, by admitting your weakness in the face of the problem, you open yourself to help from other sources. Step Three—making a decision to turn your will and life over to the care of your Higher Power—asks for that help.

Once you admit that your efforts have proven inadequate and you invoke a power greater than yourself—a

"Higher Power"—you are in the position to do what you could not do before: gain mastery over your problems.

But what Higher Power? How can you harness that power and direct it toward your recovery? And what if you don't attend church or temple, or believe in God or a Higher Power in the first place?

Stepping back

At first glance the language in the Twelve Steps suggests that you must. God is capitalized, referred to as a "He," and described as if "He" will take over and solve your problems if you just believe. If that interpretation and that view work for you, fine. Use them.

If not, look again. Consider substituting the term "Higher Power," "spirit," or "love" for God. Use language that has meaning for *you*.

In one sense your God is whatever you give yourself over to, and it can be a Higher Power or a lower power. If you have a compulsion or addiction you have already turned your daily problems over to a power greater than you, a "lower power" god, such as food, alcohol, or other people's approval. Your "Higher Power" God can be anything to which you give yourself that can enhance your life, enhance others, or enhance the world. In order to help you recover, then, Steps Two and Three ask you to align yourself with a power greater than your dependency.

Whatever your beliefs, if you can find a way to strengthen your spirituality, if you can open your life to a greater source of power than you have relied upon in the past, you can recover. Acknowledge that your dependency is bigger than you, understand that it will take a power greater than you to help you turn yourself around, and turn the problems of your life over to that Higher Power.

If you are not a believer in a religious sense, you may have a nontraditional view of God, or may be open to alternative forms of spirituality. Or perhaps you do not believe in God at all. Yet you may have an interest or focus in your life that enhances you, others, and the world. You may be an athlete. You may study dance. You may devote yourself to the service of others. So long as this consuming focus is a positive force, it is a Higher Power working in your life. A famous theologian, Paul Tillich, considers God to be simply one's "ultimate concern." Your consuming interest, the inspiration and direction it gives you, is your God.

Three Different Views

Each spiritual alignment has its own resources and issues. Perhaps one of the following perspectives applies to you.

If you already hold traditional beliefs...

Many people have had some involvement with religion while growing up. They may have moved away from church involvement, or be angry with their God, but they basically have a fairly clear concept of God. If this describes you, then you have that background to work with. Use the resources of prayer, meditation, religious writings such as the Bible or the Koran, and the fellowship of believers to assist you in your recovery.

◆ ◆ ◆

Steve, *an alcoholic, was referred to a rehabilitation program by his employer. He is having difficulties admitting he has a problem.*

Steve came to slowly. The familiar objects of his room at the condo swam into focus. The red LED numbers on his alarm clock read 11:23 A.M., and he felt like hell. Slowly, he remembered. He had checked himself out of the rehab center yesterday, prior to the end of his first week and against medical advice. But oh, how he had hated being there! He felt locked up. He had disliked the staff's condescending attitude, and his counselor had presented a constant challenge. Sharing a room had left him feeling exposed and under constant scrutiny. Knowing that he was there because his employer required it—or would fire him for cause—was embarrassing and infuriating.

All of this had been endurable with the help of the two bottles of vodka he had smuggled in, but once they were finished that it had quickly turned unbearable. It wasn't as if he was chemically dependent. But without the cushion the alcohol provided, the place was quite intolerable.

By 2:00 P.M. yesterday he was on the street. He had hit every bar between the Center and his condo with a vengeance. He wasn't sure how late he had gotten in. As he lay in bed listening to the mower he was struck with how odd it sounded. He couldn't remember ever having been home during the week to hear it.

So now what do I do? He wondered. I suppose I could just stay here until they call. But who would call? He had checked out of the program. Richard, his boss, probably still thought he was at St. John's. The implications of his actions were now settling in.

He got up, got a beer, and sat at the dining table. I could call Rich, he thought. But that would put Rich in the position of having to act. Better let him find out later. Steve ate some cereal, got another beer, and flipped on the TV.

At 9 P.M. he woke from his nap. The empty beer cans crowded the little table by his chair. Commercials on TV flashed between programs. His tongue felt thick and his head was pounding.

I've got to find some place to go, Steve thought as he got up again. He got dressed, put on a jacket, and went out to his car. No car. Then he remembered: he had left it at the bar not far from his condo and walked the three blocks. He put on a jacket and set out to the bar to reclaim the car.

On the way he passed a church. The sight made him smile. On one side of the street, the church; on the other side, a little farther down the road, was the cocktail lounge where he had ended up last night. The irony was not lost upon Steve. The church was open for vespers. It might be interesting to go in, he thought. What the hell, he shrugged, I've got time to kill.

The sanctuary was fairly empty as Steve chose a pew toward the back. He sat in the dim light, relaxing for a moment. The priest was droning on and the seats were comfortable enough.

It was funny being in the church again. The religious symbols were comforting. As a child he had loved church and loved doing church things. How easy the world had seemed back then. If only his parents hadn't separated. He remembered them leaving the church; he had been nine years old. Although he had gotten used to living without church, he had really gotten mad when they got back together and joined another church. He had refused to go. Now, sitting here in the quiet, Steve was reminded of what he had been missing.

So how was he going to get out of this mess? Absolutely nothing was working. He knew he was going to have to go back to the rehab center or lose his job, and this was not a good time to lose any job. But it was all so fake. The motivation speech the first day was humiliating. It was clear that he needed help, but it wasn't clear where he was going to get it.

He remembered another time he had taken refuge in a church. He was nineteen and had just been dumped by Lori. While their dating had been a prolonged fight, he had been undone by feelings of abandonment. During that period of disorientation and distress the church had been the one constant in his life.

Then it came to him. What he needed was right under his nose. The church. If he had the church to rely on, to sustain him again, he could get straight. It had worked for him before. It was about the only thing that had worked for him. And he knew that it would be the only thing that would work again. If he could get right with God, and get back into the church, he could handle St. John's, his job, and whatever else went wrong.

Relieved, and with a sense of satisfaction and direction, Steve left the service to get his car. He needed to make some calls.

◆ ◆ ◆

Don't be afraid or ashamed to turn your problem over to God. Many people assume that God or the church belong to the righteous, who would reject them if their problem was known. This is usually based on a belief that only "good" people go to church. A better way to view the church might be as an extended self-help group. The somewhat superior bumper-sticker that reads "Christians are not perfect, just forgiven" is true of all faiths. It is an acknowledgment of the basic human condition: that we all have flaws, and that all truly spiritual people accept that— in others and in themselves.

If you feel ashamed to enter into a relationship with the God in whom you believe and are afraid to ask for assistance, perhaps your view of others is overinflated, your view of God too punitive, or your view of yourself too harsh. Perhaps your fear of asking God for direct assistance is based on a fear of not being forgiven. And that fear may in turn be based in your not being willing to forgive yourself.

If you feel a church would not accept you if they knew about your struggles, you may be right. But check out your perceptions with someone in the church whom you trust. If your suspicions are confirmed, find a more realistic, supportive church. Be clear, however, just who is being judgmental. Before you leave, make sure that you aren't the one making the assumptions.

Some people believe in a personal God, but cannot or will not turn to God for help because they are too angry or distrustful. This often stems from early family experiences. Punitive religious training or childhood hurts associated with the church can leave bitter feelings toward God. Similarly, unrealistic promises made about God's protection followed by difficult life experiences can create feelings of betrayal, anger, or distrust. If early experiences are keeping you from a more adult, productive relationship with the God you believe in, examine your feelings. Find a competent pastoral counselor to help you sort through and reevaluate your feelings. Also, look at the suggestions for using church resources listed in the next section.

If you have a good, solid relationship with God, and if your spiritual experience is a source of strength and renewal in your life, then you have a tremendous asset in your struggle.

If you have nontraditional beliefs, or are undecided...

Some people have spiritual ideas and beliefs that do not fit most religions. Others can attend churches without having to fight the words spoken there. They can "see beyond" the language, and are able to share in the members spirituality, activities, and support.

◆ ◆ ◆

Frances, a bulimic, has been attending a Twelve Step group on the suggestion of her friend Annie. She knows she has a problem, but is not sure what she should do.

The Overeater's meeting began at 7:30, and Frances met Annie there. Some things were read, and then people introduced themselves. Most were overeaters, some were dependent upon other things. Each used just his or her first name and identified his or her particular problem.

As people shared their stories and struggles, Frances was amazed. She heard herself described over and over. The names changed, the individual circumstances changed, but the pattern of attempting to control their lives through their eating stayed the same. Pain and anxiety led to eating or starving, the eating pattern led to shame, shame led to pain and anxiety. She heard stories of triumph. Members related their experiences of overcoming the devastation of living with an eating disorder.

It was too good to be true. She wanted to believe that this was a place she could safely be, a place where she could tell about what was happening to her without being laughed at or criticized. Yet, there was something going on with which she was having trouble.

"I had to let go of it," one woman was saying, "I just had to turn it over to God." That was it, thought Frances. These people are believers. If I were a Christian, I could believe in God. But that would be a lie. I don't, and I'm not, and if that's what you have to be, then I can't.

After the meeting Frances was still troubled. "Annie, you have a faith that I just don't have. This is not going to work!" She felt the old panic returning.

"Why don't you try talking to Dr. Abrams?" Annie suggested. "She understands. Maybe she can help."

♦ ♦ ♦

The office was quiet. Dr. Abrams sat in an easy chair across from Frances, her graying hair pulled back into a loose bun. Her eyes were gently probing, and she waited for Frances to think about the question she had just asked.

Frances felt disoriented. Something about the question had thrown her. She couldn't even remember what had been asked. "Could you repeat that?"

"I asked if you believed in chaos," repeated Dr. Abrams.

"I don't understand."

"Well, some people think that things just happen without rhyme or reason. That's chaos. Others feel that there is some sort of purpose behind it all."

"I'm not sure," replied Frances. And indeed she wasn't. She had fought with her parents over religion. They were strict Catholics, and had expected Frances to accept Catholicism without question. They had been thunderstruck when she had walked out of confirmation class. "Dr. Abrams, I'm not a very religious person. I don't like church, with all its attitude and judgments. My parents wanted me to go when I was young, but it seemed so dishonest."

"So you don't believe in anything?"

"Well, I didn't say that." Frances thought some more. How could she say it? As the years had gone by she had felt a need for some sort of religion but nothing felt right.

"Frances," Dr. Abrams pushed forward "maybe you aren't a religious person, but you certainly sound like a very spiritual one to me. You seem to be looking for something. You seem to be demanding something of yourself and of the world. What do you expect?"

Ah! That's it. She couldn't imagine a world this complicated not having a reason or direction. She could not imagine a person in this world who didn't have a place and role in it. Life—her life—had to make sense. "I guess I expect there to be a reason for my being here, a meaning for my life. I expect myself to find that meaning, whatever it is, and make it happen."

"Then that search for meaning is your God, Frances."

"Even though I don't know just what it is?"

"Even though you don't have all the answers."

♦ ♦ ♦

So, thought Frances on her way home from the session. I don't have to "be religious" to be in that group. Her God could be an abstract God, and she could still believe that the group process would help. She had a mission in this world, and recovering from her bulimia was the first step in finding out what her purpose was. Dr. Abrams was good, she thought. Talking to her was helpful. She really heard me, and I think she understood.

It was decided. She would return to the support group on Thursday.

♦ ♦ ♦

If your experience is similar to Frances', you might find strength associating with a active spiritually-oriented group engaged in a search for enduring values. You may find them in a church, synagogue, or temple; you may find them elsewhere. Here are some suggestions for how could you benefit:

- more contact with members
- personal contact with the leader
- greater involvement with service and activities

- special interest or worship groups
- special projects
- specialized resources
- key people you can turn to when things are difficult for you

Give some thought to how you could find out about these opportunities and take advantage of them.

Many people have found personal rituals or devotions helpful if practiced regularly. Whatever your beliefs, by incorporating a regular spiritual practice into your program, you strengthen your spiritual self and provide yourself with power for change. Think about ways to develop regular practices which would be meaningful to you. The key will be to design your own, which fit your beliefs and life. Become a spiritual scientist, trying different approaches and testing them against your own experience.

We often get "set in our ways" spiritually as well as in other values and beliefs. This sometimes happens at one stage in our lives, and then does not change along with our growth in other areas. This might be a perfect time to explore, reexamine, and develop new spiritual beliefs and expressions. Who could you talk to about this? And how can you experiment with turning problems over to the spirit you acknowledge, and incorporate your searching and discoveries into your efforts at recovery?

Many communities have secular activities and resources available that are not church related but can be helpful in developing personal spirituality. Some suggestions are provided in the next section. Consider exploring these as well.

And if you do not believe...

Others are not ready for acknowledging any sort of spiritual power outside of themselves. When faced with a seemingly overwhelming compulsion or addiction, they often "cave-in" quickly to the same feelings of inadequacy and paralysis that you may be feeling.

If this describes you, you might try answering the following question: Haven't you already turned over your own life to a power greater than yourself?

♦ ♦ ♦

Elizabeth is a codependent. She is desperate to be loved and continually suffers abuse in shallow and unrewarding relationships. She sabotages her own efforts at attaining the goals which she desires. She has just been to her first Codependents Anonymous meeting.

"You know, Tina, it's ironic. I want nothing more than to make these things work and they keep blowing up in my face. I don't know. Something's wrong and I just can't figure out what it is. I don't drink, I don't use drugs, I don't have any of the normal 'problems,' yet I somehow mess up every relationship I'm in." Elizabeth and Tina were walking down the street after a CodA meeting. It was Saturday and people were milling around the local bars and cafes.

"I don't know when to stop. I choose the wrong people and let myself get dumped on. No one seems to like me anymore. I'm frantic trying to get people to like me, and I get nowhere. Tina, you don't seem to work at it. You seem lit up from the inside. How do you do it?"

"Elizabeth, I'm not always happy. And I don't have all that many good friends. I was a lot like you—am a lot like you. But I've learned that I have to like myself first or no amount of friends will be enough."

"How do you learn to like yourself?" asked Elizabeth. In my case, she wondered to herself, what's to like?

"It took a while," said Tina. "I learned a lot through the CoDa group, and the help of a couple of good friends. I had to learn that I was good enough the way I was. I used to think that I had to do the things that other people wanted. I was afraid of losing their love and approval if I didn't. I never considered that they might have to win mine."

"But people won't like you if you don't make them happy," tried Elizabeth.

"It depends upon who it is. Elizabeth, I like you whether or not you get over depending upon others. I would hope that you can get strong and stop holding others up to be God, but I'm not going to like you any more or less because of it."

Tina held the door of the cafe open for Elizabeth. They found a booth, sat down, and ordered.

As they waited for their lunch, Elizabeth looked troubled. "Just now you said something that puzzled me. What do you mean 'holding others up to be God'?"

"Well," answered Tina, "if you see other people as more important than you are, and you take their wishes to be your commands, it sounds like you believe that they are gods."

"But I don't really believe in any God," protested Elizabeth.

"You act like it. Everybody has a God. With some people it's the biblical God, with some it's their work, and with some it's a bottle. With you it's other people."

Elizabeth thought about it. "What's your God?"

Tina looked straight at her. "This might not make sense to you, but my God is my own Higher Self."

"What's that?" asked Elizabeth, who thought she might already know.

"For me, my Higher Self is the part of me that knows what is right or wrong, that knows what's really best for me.

It's who I am growing to be. Since I started going to the CoDA group I have been developing that part of me."

My Higher Self, thought Elizabeth. A God within. As she walked down to her car, Elizabeth thought about the discussion. All her life Elizabeth had looked for a Higher Power. She looked for God in others, because she couldn't believe in herself. But it was getting very obvious that looking to others was not working for her. Elizabeth was getting ready for a new way of looking at things.

◆ ◆ ◆

Elizabeth, not believing in a religious god, has nonetheless assigned higher powers to everyone but herself in an effort to be accepted and loved. As she works on loving and trusting herself, she finds her spiritual higher power to be the part of herself that knows what is destructive and what is fulfilling for her. Elizabeth's spirituality needs to recognize a higher sense of self to find meaning.

If you don't believe in God or some other form of spirituality, and you have been trying to turn over your daily problems to some lower power such as a compulsion or an addictive habit, you seem to have painted yourself into a corner. Your compulsion or addiction is bigger than you, but it's the only other game in town. Sounds pretty bleak.

Ponder this: you can open yourself to your *own* spirituality without holding other's beliefs. You can let yourself trust in your own Higher Power, the spirit that is within you, without having to admit the existence of an "outside" God. Instead of having to adopt the spiritual doctrines of others, you can become an investigator of your own Higher Power. You can learn to recognize the difference between your willfulness—which keeps you in bondage to your compulsion or addiction—and the quiet life-sustaining power of your own Higher Self.

Spend some time getting acquainted with your higher self. Look over the suggestions in the two previous sections. Many of them can be adapted for those without theological beliefs. In addition, many nonchurch-related community resources are available. They do not preach any specific doctrine, and can be very helpful spiritually. In particular, you are likely to find the following helpful:

- self-help groups
- service groups
- yoga classes
- Twelve-Step recovery groups
- special spiritually oriented individuals with whom you can connect
- spiritually oriented therapy groups
- recovery and spiritual literature

Sometimes you may have to translate the language. When they say "God," you say "my Higher Self." Remind yourself that using the words God or spirit serves the same function for others that "Higher Self" does for you. You are not giving anything away.

Another helpful strategy is to surround yourself with healthy people, not people who are into their lower selves, their compulsions or addictions, in order to cope. Stick with people who have tuned into their higher selves.

Remember your own vulnerability, however. Without an external Higher Power, your recovery is much more delicate. A major trap awaits those whose Higher Power is limited to their Higher Self. The trap consists of their own willfulness and the power of denial and self-deception.

It is very easy to simply return to a variation of your old way of coping, and be convinced it is an act of the Higher Self. The error consists in underestimating the power of your own disease.

Check out your motives. One way is to ask yourself: why am I doing this? Is there any way that this could simply be my old problem resurfacing? If I were to set up a personal review process, who could I use as reviewers?

Developing a Plan for Engaging Your Higher Power

In order to overcome a problem that is bigger than you are, you need help. Steps Two and Three recognize this and invite you to develop your relationship with a Higher Power. To do this you need a plan. This plan must be one you develop yourself, although you might get some suggestions from the preceding sections.

Your plan should aim at deepening your relationship with your Higher Power by including:

- specific groups and organizations that can provide spiritual resources appropriate to your beliefs and needs
- particular people who can serve as spiritual guides to whom you can an turn when you need help
- reading, study, and discussion experiences that can challenge you to grow spiritually
- rituals, meditations, or reflection experiences that can assist you in directly experiencing your own spirituality

- ways in which you can practice turning over daily problems and difficulties to your Higher Power
- strategies you can employ to avoid the willfulness/denial trap

It is also helpful to create a personal review process. Develop several trusted friends who know how you operate; know both your higher and lower sides. Write out your plan and share it with them. They can assist you in holding to it, and be a valuable support during moments of weakness and trial. Before you set new courses or when you have to cope with heavy stress, at preplanned intervals sit down with your reviewers and get their opinions as to your actions. The key to this is your choice of friends. If you pick people who will not be honest and confrontational, or people who will enable you to remain dysfunctional, it won't work. You also have to listen to the results, and take them seriously. If you play games, cover up, or ignore their concerns, you will sabotage yourself.

A personalized spirituality is a central, pivotal aspect of recovery. Without spiritual grounding, our frail powers of ego and will are constantly threatened with collapse in the face of compulsion or addiction. And there is more at stake than just abstinence.

As Sherry Hoyt found out, recovery was only the starting point in a larger reorganization of her life. Rediscovering her inspirations was the guiding force behind the new life she developed after recovery. You too will find, if you haven't already, that a more comprehensive spirituality is integral to the larger project of reclaiming your future.

2

Know Thyself...

Through the course of an addictive disease we usually spend so much time and energy in ignoring, denying, or covering up our own behavior that we lose sight of who we are. A radical step must be taken. We must not only acknowledge that our problem exists, but come to understand how big it is and how it has affected us and those around us. Only then can we take the steps necessary for healing to occur.

The following sections provide ideas, lists, strategies for self-reflection and support as you carry out a personal inventory. They highlight special issues to consider as you confront and prepare to change compulsive behavior.

Step Four asks you to make a searching and fearless moral inventory of yourself. This brings to light the type and size of your addiction. It is a model of healing that applies to wounds of the soul: holding one's life up to the air and sunlight of a searching and honest examination. Through this self-assessment you set the direction for your own treatment.

An inventory can help you understand why you do the things you do. It can assist you in recognizing when your problem cycle is self-destructive. It helps you confront your own denial and cover-ups. Step Four allows you to understand and Step Five to admit the pain you have caused others, which in turn reduces your sense of guilt. You are brought back into harmony with the world, with others around you, and with yourself.

◆ ◆ ◆

Sean is a cocaine addict and occasionally binges on alcohol. After his habit got him into court twice, he enrolled voluntarily in a detox program. Sean expected to "cure" his habit, but is finding the program focuses less on his habit and more on his whole way of life.

"Sean, who do you think you are? Better yet, who are you, really?" It was Vicki, the same woman who had been so confrontational before. "You talk a good line, but I don't see the commitment."

Everyone has a cross to bear, thought Sean. This Vicki woman seems to be mine. He fought a flash of anger. He had been in the hospital program for three weeks now, and she was really beginning to get to him. He allowed himself the luxury of an acid response. "I suppose there's some reason why you're picking on me, although it eludes me. I'm here, I work, and that should speak for itself. I'm not sure what else you want from me, but you might ask yourself whether it's really me you want it from."

Stung by his remark, Vicki rallied again. "You're right! My problems do get in the way. Maybe I didn't get what I needed from the men in my life. But that doesn't mean I'm mistaken. I try to accept my limitations and I share who I am. You don't!"

Sean was angry, but he held his tongue. He sensed that to go further would open up things he wasn't ready for yet.

After the group, Sean went back to his room to read until dinner. She's right, he thought. But I really should have let her have it.

Damn! he thought. How many times have I done that? I hold back till I can't take it anymore and then I blow up. As he began to calm down, Sean thought back and replayed similar situations in his mind. He remembered what each had cost him. Lost friends, lost jobs, lost chances, all for sixty seconds of satisfaction. Once in a while it had been worth it, but most of the time it had brought him nothing but grief. It was like a drug.

That's what coke and alcohol do for me, he thought. I get to blow off without messing up anyone else...except me.

♦ ♦ ♦

"So where did you learn you had to fight so much?" Sean hated it when shrinks turned an answer into an obvious question, and then acted so smug about it.

"When I grew up, fighting ran in my family."

"What would you do when your parents fought?"

Acted normally, Sean thought to himself, they were always fighting. "Kept out of the way, mostly. The problem was when they were making up."

"How so?"

"They were always expecting me to act as if everything was fine and that nothing happened." Sean could remember his parents both smiling at him, and both looking like they had stomach pain they didn't want to admit to having.

"How did that make you feel?"

"I felt like hitting them, except that I felt like it would be wrong."

"So, they expected you to do as they did," summarized the therapist, "make happy and act as if everything was fine when it wasn't."

"Right."

"And now?" the therapist prompted.

"What?"

"And now how are you feeling about your parents; are they still alive?"

"Yes. I don't know," answered Sean. "I mostly ignore them, and the times I see them, they're OK."

"How about now?" the therapist kept up. "How do you feel about them since you have been in this program?"

Sean was quiet, but his face was red and the veins stood out from his neck.

"Do you think," the therapist gently asked, "that the pressure your parents put on you to conform to their wishes when you were a child might have something to do with your reactions to the group?"

Owning Up

Inventories are simply the process of discovering what you need. How do you do such an inventory? It isn't easy, but it is straightforward. You ask yourself some important questions, think about them long and hard, and answer them as seriously and honestly as you can. You start with what you have done, then why you did it, and then think about what you were trying to get (something that you needed then), then what you need now, then what keeps you from getting it (why you can't change)....

What you have done

Describe, in as much detail as you can, the things you are doing that have gotten you in trouble. You must go deep, however, and look at the way in which your compulsion or addiction has made things worse for you and how your attempts to correct it have failed in the past. Consider specific actions you have taken that have caused hurt, bitterness, and fear, or separation. Make a list of incidents, specifying what you did and who was hurt. Indicate when it happened by approximate date or time frame (i.e., "November, 1983" or "when I was 13"). This list will serve as the basic "inventory" from which you can develop your recovery strategies.

Here are some direct questions you can ask yourself about your compulsion or addiction. This is a time to be completely honest with yourself. Consider getting a notebook and writing down your answers. If for any reason you are unsure of your ability to be objective, find someone whom you trust and who knows you well. Ask that person how he or she would answer the questions about you. Respect those answers.

- Do you engage in cover-ups? Have you hidden evidence? Lied?

- How have you felt doing that?

- How has your problem behavior violated your own personal standards?

- Have you experienced shame, embarrassment, or guilt for what you are doing?

- Do you find yourself doing things that you do not want to do?

- Have you lost things that are important to you (such as money, possessions, jobs, or relationships) due to your problem? List them.

- How has your problem behavior affected those whom you love (spouse, significant other, children, extended family)?

- How has it affected your job or career?

- How has it affected your social life, or the social life of your family?
- Have you gotten to the place where you are afraid you cannot stop?
- Are you afraid of doing what it would take to end your compulsion or addiction?

Think about each time you tried to change your behavior in the past. Did you try the same ways each time? Did you use any special techniques? Were you involved in any programs?

- What have you tried so far to solve this problem?
- How did it work?
- What goes wrong with your attempts to change?
- What would it take for you to admit that you had "bottomed out," or that your life had become unmanageable?
- Has it happened yet?

Working through denial is so difficult, and there is so much to learn and understand that you will probably want to return and reread this chapter at various times. Be sure to work more on your answers to these questions as your knowledge and strength increase.

Expectations and Investments

Are you in tune yet with how some of your past experiences may have shaped your current expectations?

Sometimes expectations are triggered off by being in certain places. If you had bad experiences in school as a child, it is quite possible that you now feel uncomfortable and defensive in school settings. The school setting reminds you of the difficulties of the past, and triggers off expectations that the present situation is also going to create discomfort and hurt.

Expectations can hurt in three ways. First, other people's expectations of you can limit you. Second, acting on their expectations, others can pressure you into your compulsion or addiction, or some other behavior. Third, your expectations of others can limit you.

How your expectations of yourself can limit you:

- If you feel that you will fail, you probably will
- If you feel that the only way you can cope is to engage in your problem behavior, you probably will

How your expectations of others can limit you:

- If you feel others won't like you, you will probably act in unlikable ways
- If you expect that others will hurt you or let you down, you will probably not give them a chance to prove you wrong

Present company not excepted

Another thing that keeps you from changing may be the company you keep. When you are faltering you need to surround yourself with people who can help you make it, not people who will help you fail again. When you are weak, and feel ready to toss in the towel and take a drink, go an eating binge, or blow up at people, whatever it is that you want to do, that is *not* the time to have a "friend" come up and say, "What the hell, let's do it!"

Consider your friends and family members. Who is good for you and who will feed your problem? While it is hard to do, you may find that you have to limit the time you spend with certain friends or family members.

Dependencies

The thing that keeps you from changing may be a dependency. There are two kinds: one is physical dependency. If you have been using substances like alcohol or drugs you may be physically dependent. This means that your efforts to quit will create physical cravings for the substance your body has gotten used to having. Some people can break a physical dependency "cold turkey," but it is usually difficult and often requires medical assistance.

The other kind of dependency is psychological. This one is worse. Physical dependencies are difficult to break in the short run, but psychological dependencies are harder in the long run. Many people complete a thirty day dependency recovery program, suffer through withdrawal, get clean, and then go back to their addiction because they cannot cope psychologically without using. We become psychologically addicted to using drugs, to abusing food, or to entering unhealthy relationships because these actions help us cope in the short run.

If you want to change yourself you are going to have to change the influences around you. You are going to have to challenge you own expectations and become aware of when you are setting yourself up for defeat. You are going to have to take your dependencies seriously and act upon them. They will not go away by themselves. And finally, you are going to have to sort through your friends, and get rid of the dead wood that drags you down. Friends who help destroy you are worse than no friends at all.

Gains and Losses

It may help to conceptualize your problem differently. Problems usually run in cycles. Something triggers the cycle, the compulsion or addiction takes over, and the situation gets worse. This happens in two ways. By using an addiction to cope, Sean made things worse off than they were before. The coping style provided temporary relief from the immediate stress, but increased stress in the long run. Even worse, Sean never learned to handle the difficult situation in the first place, and now he is faced with finding alternatives.

Problems are circular because each stage leads to the next, and so the cycle tends to perpetuate itself. Yet something powers it, or it would just fizzle out.

The cycle is powered by investment. Just as we take care of things we pay a lot for, we protect those things in which we have invested much time and energy, and from which we benefit. In order to break a problem cycle it is first necessary to find out what we gain from it, then find better ways to get those benefits.

Perhaps by drinking you are able to extinguish anxiety. Perhaps by starting family fights you are able to avoid making difficult changes in the relationship. Perhaps by putting off difficult assignments you are able to get out of being judged by others.

Take a few hours (or a few days!) to think about what

you have to gain by *not* changing. What's in it for you to continue the cycle you get into? It is often hard to look at your own motives this way, but try.

Start by looking at the overall problem you have decided to overcome. What sorts of gains might you have been enjoying as a result of doing it? Consider the following possibilities:

- a quick "rush" or "high"
- avoidance of something worse
- dealing with difficult feelings
- avoiding some challenge
- a way of sending a message
- controlling some other person
- denying a painful change
- controlling fear or anxiety
- avoiding a serious risk
- putting off taking care of some other business
- feeling at least some control in a difficult situation
- living out someone else's idea of how you should be
- something else: _____

Sometimes it's hard to figure out why we keep doing something that is bad for us. Usually it's because we are getting something out of doing it. This is called "secondary gain." Secondary gain is often difficult to identify because the cycle of undesirable behavior seems so damaging and the gain seems so small. Other times it is hard to understand because the gain is complex and subtle.

If you have been able to identify a gain or two that you get from the problem behavior, think about the underlying needs which those secondary gains satisfy. It may be easier to find a more healthy and direct way to meet these needs. For example, if you drink to avoid anxiety, then the underlying need might be to feel secure. If you work on other ways to increase your sense of security, such as joining a support group or special interest group, you will find it easier to keep from drinking.

But while you are adding up the secondary gains from your problem behavior you should also weigh those gains against your losses. Your problem—be it drinking, eating, drugs, running away, or relationship addiction—has caused you grief. You may have lost friends, money, jobs, or personal property through your mismanagement or need to feed your habit. Let's take inventory of those losses. As a result of your problem, have you

- lost money?
- lost personal property?
- lost friends?
- lost control?
- lost respect?
- lost your sense of identity?

Are the losses which you have suffered worth the secondary gains? Are these losses tolerable? If your problem behavior continues its present course, what do you stand to lose in the future?

Cover ups

Denial was a particularly important problem for Sean. His denial, along with his anger, kept him from benefiting from his recovery program. He avoided conflicts with other patients. But this pattern was not new to him. He had been running to drugs and hiding there for some time. Facing up to things directly was Sean's biggest need in recovery.

In order to maintain our addiction or compulsion, we often cover up our behavior, hiding it from others as well as ourselves. We do this so we won't get caught, won't be confronted, won't have to change.

Think about the following cover-up strategies. Do you see yourself in any of them?

hiding evidence	lying	cover stories
explanations	justifications	rationalization
alibi	blaming	denial
displaced anger	smokescreens	exaggeration
minimization	stealing	other: _____

Even if these were really working, the effect would only be to keep you malfunctioning. And they might not even be working as well as you think. A great many people may be seeing right through your attempts, and your problem might already have gone public.

Deception is demeaning. We are embarrassed by our problem and by our attempts to cover up. As a result of our losses of self-control and self-respect and our attempts at cover up through lies and deception, we often end up harboring deep feelings of shame. As our lives become less and less manageable, we become more and more embarrassed. Our dignity is compromised.

Think about the shame you feel. If you were to rate

how bad it was on a ten-point scale, how would you rate it? Think about what it would be like to be shame-free right now. Would you have to change in your life to be shame-free?

Confiding in Others

As you work with your self-assessment, you might wish to choose someone with whom to share your questioning. This is the fundamental aspect of Step Five, admitting to another human being the exact nature of your wrongs. Because we so easily deceive ourselves into believing the best or worst, someone else's opinion can be helpful. Not just anyone, however. Opinions are only as good as their sources. Think about the people in your life. Some don't really know you, and some have problems worse than yours. Whose opinion can you trust?

Call these people feedback sources, because they will feed back their reactions to you about whether or not they feel your answers are honest and accurate. Caution! Do not pick someone who has the same problem you are trying to overcome! That person may have a more distorted view than yours, or be in a worse position than you to be honest or objective.

While working through the exercises in this section, consider asking your feedback sources to review your answers with you. This may be hard. You have to let them know how important it is that they be honest, even if it means hurting your feelings or offending you.

Also, because taking on this challenge is very difficult, you will need support in your efforts. You or your feedback sources may be discussing things that are painful. You will need someone else to talk to who can listen to you when you are tired, depressed, or angry. Think about someone who could give you that kind of support.

Getting What You Want

The following steps may help you prepare yourself to get what you want out of recovery.

- Review the list of secondary gains you compiled on page 39. These are the things you stand to lose by turning yourself around.

- Review the alternative ways you have of satisfying these needs. These are ways to minimize the losses you stand to suffer by the changes you are attempting to make.

- Review the losses you have already suffered as a result of not turning yourself around, including money, property, friends, control, respect, and identity.

- Review the losses you believe you will continue to suffer if you do not change.

Think about the answers you have given in this section. If you choose to change, you will live with one set of consequences. If you choose not to change, you will live with another set of consequences.

The following are shortcomings that make recovery difficult and may be hurtful to others.

helplessness	explosiveness	dishonesty
defensiveness	impatience	rage
impulsiveness	distrust	destructiveness

irresponsibility fear   jealousy
perfectionism   false pride false humility
other: _____

Consider those that apply to you. These traits are hard enough for you to live with. Think how they impact your family, friends, and co-workers.

Traits are enduring personal characteristics. So are attitudes. It is normal to have negative feelings, but feelings are generally short lived. Having negative attitudes is different, however. Attitudes persist, and they shape how we see and respond to others. The following abusive attitudes can make recovery difficult and can be hurtful to others.

resentment   contempt   paranoia
arrogance   pessimism   intolerance
patronage   intolerance criticism
skepticism   envy   judgment
moralism   distrust   self-centeredness
unforgiving   aloofness   punitiveness

Traits and attitudes are often difficult to see in ourselves. Have you ever been accused of any of these behaviors by a family member or friend? Were you receptive to the claim, or did you brush it off as just part of an argument? Think again. Perhaps it might be time to reapproach that person and explore how he or she really experiences you. Who else could you go to for feedback? Consider how you might approach those people in order to get honest answers. Would the same person you read your inventory to be the best one with whom to check out your perceptions about your attitudes?

One of the hardest things is to look clearly at ourselves—and not reject what we see. For recovery to be successful, however, objective self-assessment is an unceasing process. The great gift of self-assessment is that, as you come to know yourself better, you will get in touch with your humanness, admit your frailty and acknowledge your greatness. Inevitably, this leads away from self-hatred —the cause of many of our problems—to self-acceptance, even self-love, and acceptance and deep love of others.

3

Creative Amends

Whatever caused your problem in the first place, whatever kept it alive, and whatever pain it brought you, one thing is certain. In the course of your suffering, your behavior caused others pain, for which you are responsible.

Whenever we bring pain to others, we put ourselves off balance. Our actions cut two ways: we cause pain to the ones we hurt, and in doing so, we lose our own sense of integrity. We experience guilt and shame for our wrongdoing, and these are painful to us. If we are to gain peace of mind—the very thing we need to recover from our compulsion or addiction—we must right the wrongs we have committed.

With the possible exception of sociopaths or persons whose developmental disabilities preclude normal human functioning, we are all moral. We maintain a fairly consistent understanding of right and wrong. When we act in immoral ways, violating our own standards of right action, the feelings of imbalance increase and our self-esteem is diminished. When we have histories of bringing hurt to others we carry a burden of pervasive guilt. We feel cut off from others and cut off from our Higher Self—isolated from a respectful, meaningful life.

Settling your social accounts lifts this burden from your shoulders. Owning up to your past actions and accepting responsibility for their consequences allows you to ask forgiveness from others and to forgive yourself. You are set free to grow fully into the future.

Step Eight urges you to make a list of all persons you have harmed, and become willing to make amends to them all. Making amends is one of the most powerful tools you have to turn around your problem behavior. Through the amend-making process you defuse the shame which constricts you, set the stage for reconstructing healthy relationships, and open yourself to a future full of new possibilities.

Step Nine requires making direct amends—actual apology and restitution—to such people wherever possible, except when to do so would injure them or others.

This chapter explores how to go about righting past wrongs, how to straighten out your relationships, and how to put them back on a sane footing. It offers you realistic procedures for assessing and making amends when simple or straightforward apologies won't work. This task is creative and personal. Because of the differences in the people wronged, the different types of wrong, and the uniqueness of each situation, each person must discover her or his own way.

♦ ♦ ♦

Tamiko, a fashion designer, is an anorexic. She has been in a recovery program for two years. Since working on family issues with Dr. Abrams, Tamiko had been reevaluating many things about herself, her family, and her relationship with her fairly traditional Japanese parents.

Tamiko had let go of much of the anger she held against her parents and their culture, and had gotten to the point of even forgiving them for not seeing her as an individual. She was coming to understand they had their own very real limitations. She was healing—but they were not. She was moving forward with her recovery and rebuilding her relationships. And yet, try as she might, her parents just were not ready. "Maybe they are still hanging on to the past," Tamiko tried.

"Maybe it's something else," suggested Dr. Abrams.

"Like what?"

"Like maybe they are angry with you."

"Because I moved out to live alone?" asked Tamiko.

"Perhaps. But it might be simpler than that. Maybe something more subtle."

♦ ♦ ♦

"Come on, Tami!" urged Beth. "Of course you know why they're mad." They were walking under the camphor trees that lined the street near the park. The recent rain made the leaves slippery and the air sweet. "How many times have you told me about how you shut people out and hold back? Don't you think you did that to them too?"

"But Beth," Tamiko protested, "I had to. Look at the way they treated me... all those expectations. First they tell me I have to have a career and do well. So I spend six years in fashion school and get a career. And as soon as I'm doing well they want me to marry and settle down—and you *know* they're thinking Japanese. So I'm just supposed to become the perfect wife, have children, and forget about my career. Well there's just no way I'm going to do that!" She realized she was practically yelling.

They waited for a light to change. "You know, Tami," said Beth, "I'm not saying that they did anything right. But look at it from their side. Nobody's perfect. They worked hard at raising you, and you grow up angry at them. Then you start withdrawing and shut them out. How do you expect them to feel?"

The light changed, and they crossed.

I wonder what would happen, Tamiko mused, if I was to just suddenly tell them what was going on. The thought was so unsettling she almost tripped over the curb.

♦ ♦ ♦

Tamiko's parents' home felt comfortably familiar. They had been surprised at her forcefulness when she called and said she needed to talk with both of them. They sat on the couch and she sat on a chair opposite. She wished she had tea to pour or something to do with her hands.

"What's the matter, Tamiko?" asked her father. He was not used to her taking the lead.

"Thank you for sitting down with me." Tamiko had rehearsed this several times, but it still felt awkward. "I have some things I need to tell you. I've ... "

"Tami," asked her mother, with a worried look, "are you in some kind of trouble? Is everything all right?"

Tamiko laughed nervously. "No, everything's not alright. I mean, well, I guess I have been in trouble for a few years." Her parents looked more confused than ever. "You see, I discovered two years ago that I am an anorexic."

Confusion changed to shock. "What do you mean ... " began her father.

"It's an eating disorder. I starve myself because I'm afraid of becoming fat—and the doctor says there may be other reasons." She went on to explain.

"Tami, we didn't know!" her mother exclaimed.

"No, you didn't know because I kept it from you. In fact, that's the main reason I need to talk to you. During the past few years I've been hiding a lot from you."

Her father's eyes narrowed with suspicion. "This is because you work too hard, isn't it?"

"No," Tamiko said. "This is because of me. I have driven

a wedge between us. I'm terribly sorry. Through my withdrawal from you, I kept you from knowing your daughter."

◆ ◆ ◆

Eduard *is a recovering alcoholic. He works with a therapist to get feedback and direction during his recovery program.*

The late afternoon sun warmed Dr. Wheeler's office. "How is the 'amends business' going, Eduard?" he asked, leaning back and playing with a pencil.

"It's strange," Eduard said. "I've been going out for breakfast with my team leaders. That's working great! We're growing closer. But I just can't bring myself to apologize to my parents. And there's this woman in marketing..."

"Let's start with your parents," Dr. Wheeler interjected.

"I think I'd rather talk about the woman in marketing."

"I'm sure you would," smiled Dr. Wheeler. "What's up with your parents?"

"I don't know. I do know that my drinking and messing up in high school hurt them a lot, especially my mother. Dad told me that, and I am sorry I hurt her. When I finished school I didn't feel very comfortable around them, so we saw less and less of each other. Lately I haven't talked to either of them. Every time I go to call them, something sticks in my throat and I just can't do it. I can't make that call."

"Maybe you're still too mad at her," suggested Dr. Wheeler.

"What do you mean?"

"Well, we've talked a lot about the way she and your dad would shut you out when they were having problems and then act like nothing was wrong. You mentioned that they would expect you to pretend you were just one big happy family, when really you weren't. Yet you seem to be better able to forgive your father for his shortcomings. Why not your mom? Did she do something especially hurtful to you? Is there something there you just can't forgive yet?"

Eduard thought for a bit. The sunlight was fading now as twilight set in, and the room was growing darker. "You know," he said slowly, "there was one thing. When my mom and dad would be fighting, and I would do something bad, Mom would dump on me." He grew more intense as he got clearer as to what it all meant. "She would throw up her hands and yell 'There, see? You're just like your father.' To her that meant bad, a bum, irresponsible. God, I hated that!"

"So why was that so bad?"

"Because of the way she felt about him. It meant that she felt I was nothing but a problem. I couldn't do anything right. If it wasn't for me, everything would be OK." He thought for a minute more. "That I was nothing but a drunk."

Dr. Wheeler reached over and turned on the desk lamp. "As I said, it sounds to me like you are still too mad to ask her forgiveness. It would mean caving in and admitting she was right in all that she implied when she was mad."

Eduard was quiet. His mother's implications may have been wrong, but Dr. Wheeler's were right. He needed to make amends to his mother to clear away old resentments. Recovery required it. But he would have to start by forgiving her for her shortcomings if he was going to be able to make amends for his.

◆ ◆ ◆

By acknowledging the harm they have done in the past, Tamiko and Eduard free themselves for their future. Tamiko melts the frozen relationship with her parents and Eduard lets go of his fight with his family. They have unburdened themselves inside and begun healing their relationships with family and friends.

Through her discussion with Dr. Abrams, Tamiko came to understand how her behavior had created a deeper rift with her parents than she had realized. Later she recognized other relationships that had been affected by her actions. Knowing that she needed to make amends, she decided to talk to her family directly.

Eduard had a similar experience when amends to his father led to the discovery that his mother had been more seriously affected. He had difficulty making amends to her, however, and learned through Dr. Wheeler the extent of his anger. He was in no position to make amends until he had come to grips with that anger.

In the process of making amends, each discovered the extent of harm she or he had done. Each learned more about her- or himself. And each worked out his or her own way to rebalance the social scales. Amend-making was necessary to them, and is necessary to you, to pave the way toward recovery and healthy relationships.

If you are going to settle past accounts, if you are going to make amends for past wrongs, do it right! Take the time to figure out just what is was you did and how best to apologize and make restitution. You will probably be nervous, and you may even put off doing it to avoid embarrassment or humiliation. But just remember: you have as much or more to gain as the person to whom you will apologize.

If you can't bring yourself to make direct amends, or to do so would be imprudent, find a way to make indirect amends and carry them out. They are necessary to your self-awareness and your peace of mind.

Take the process seriously, and you will get serious results.

What Happened?

There are many ways we can hurt people. Here's a partial list of offenses against others:

intolerance	embarrassment
helplessness	stealing
jealousy	abuse
immorality	irresponsibility
fights	exploding
dishonesty	constant arguing
insults	name-calling
overcommitment	displaced anger
withdrawal	controlling behavior
demands	self-centeredness
breaking promises	

We all have done some of the above things. Some of us have done all of them. Often nothing comes of it, but sometimes we do real harm. You probably don't need to make amends for every offense against another person, but there are incidents which have been particularly hurtful. These require action in order to clear your conscience and your relationships.

From the list above, search back in your memories for specific incidents. Think about when they occurred, who was involved, and what you did. Remember that it is easy to forget incidents and to underestimate the harm you have done. Take the time you need to explore your own memories and talk to others about your actions in the past. Talk to relatives or friends who have known you for a long time. Tell them about your recovery and ask them if they can recall incidents in which you were hurtful to others. Be particularly open to their comments and perspectives about the effects of your actions. It is easy to forget things about which you are not proud.

As you remember or learn about incidents, make notes on each. Make an estimate of the damage you think you did to that person. Think about damage inflicted at that time, damage that surfaced later, and the way in which the incident damaged your relationship over time and even up until the present. There are three types of current pain caused by past actions:

- the victim of your hurtful actions may still be experiencing pain
- we may be experiencing shame
- your relationship together may be impaired

Consider devoting space in a notebook for organizing your amend-making, in the format below:

....

Incident #1 Approximate date of incident: _____
Who was involved: _____

What I did: _____

What damage I did: _____

....

Do this for about six or seven incidents.

Amends

Once you have a list of incidents requiring amends, your work is cut out for you. You have created an inventory of people with whom you need to get clear. While this list may grow as you recall incidents or learn about pain you have caused, you have a starting point. It is time to decide how and when to make the amends to those on your list.

How you make amends will vary according to who you are, who you need to make amends to, the incident, and the way things stand at the present. The apology consists in acknowledging what occurred and accepting responsibility for having done it. It lets the other person know it was not his or her fault. Apologies restore the personal dignity of the person who was hurt, as well as your own.

Restitution consists of attempts to pay back for damages. Some damages are to property, in which case fixing or replacing damaged property, or paying money may be appropriate. Some damages are irreplaceable, and you may find sometimes time or effort can be acceptable as partial restitution. Because each situation differs, you may need to be very creative in the ways you make restitution. Symbolic restitution is important to both of you even if full payback is impossible.

Sometimes making amends can cause further harm. Normally, amend-making includes a full disclosure of the incident. But if full disclosure would hurt the recipient more, hurt a third party unnecessarily, cause family turmoil, damage reputations, or in any way be harmful, then it should not be made.

In such cases a partial disclosure may be possible. Partial disclosure includes only that information necessary for the apology, or only the part of the information which is not hurtful. In cases where information must be left out, restitution can best be made by more loving, considerate, and responsible behavior.

Indirect amends

In cases where amends would be hurtful it is better not to make them. Rather than deprive yourself of this healing process, though, find an indirect alternative. This can be accomplished alone or with other, noninvolved people present. Here are some alternatives to direct amends:

By Yourself

- Sit in front of an empty chair. Close your eyes and imagine the person to whom you need to make amends sitting opposite you. Say what you would have said had that person really been there. Imagine the response. Talk with that person.

- Imagine yourself before a group. Give a speech to them, in which you disclose your actions and make amends.

- Talk to a picture of the person.

- Write a letter to the person. You can decide later whether or not to mail it.

- Write a dialogue with the person. Write your amends as if you were saying them, and write responses you think he or she might make.

- Write a dialogue with the entire incident itself.

- Imagine, act, or write enlargements or extensions of the incident or of your making amends. Carry it into the future.

With Others

- Act out the incident, including stopping your actions, and apologizing and making restitution on the spot.

♦ Role play your amend-making, using a stand-in to play the part of the person whom you injured.

Through Service An excellent way to make indirect amends is through service. Amends by works are acts you perform that make restitution for your past actions. While you may never utter the words "I'm sorry," you acknowledge your responsibility through these works. The specific service you make should be appropriate to the actions you committed.

Look back at the exercise on page 54 where you examined the hurt that each of your actions caused. For each incident, consider whether payback would help either you or the injured party; what would it feel like to receive and give restitution? Finally, consider whether the restitution needs to be in full, partial, or simply some token.

Consider devoting additional notebook space for planing amends. The figure on the next page shows a model for planning amends. You may not need to follow such a norm for most, but for the most significant or problematic situations it might be helpful.

The point of making amends is to clear the books in your relationships. Acknowledgement, apology, and restitution free the relationship and free the self from the bonds of the past. They open the future for a new sense of freedom, new ways of relating, and new possibilities.

The amend-making process is never over. It is a fundamental building block to good relationships. Because you are human you will continue to make mistakes and hurt others. Learning to incorporate amend-making as an on-going part of living gives you the power to maintain a healthy support system for yourself.

As you make amends, you begin to see people as outside you. You are no longer responsible for them, what

....

Incident #1
Plan for apology: _____

_____

Plan for restitution: _____

_____

Alternative, indirect apology if necessary: _____

_____

Date of amend-making: _____

_____

How I felt: _____

_____

His or her reaction: _____

_____

What I learned: _____

_____

Other amends necessary: _____

_____

....

they do, how they behave. You begin to see and value them for what they are. As you lose the fear that you will somehow abuse them you begin to develop more spontaneous, free, and loving relationships.

4

Managing Stress, Preventing a Relapse

Most of us have heard that "once an alcoholic, always an alcoholic." This does not mean that an alcoholic will always drink. But it does mean that once a person has become addicted to alcohol, drying out does not guarantee that he or she will never become addicted again. The possibility of relapse is ever-present. Recovery is never forever; it is always accomplished and maintained one day at a time.

Many people in recovery discover that when things are not right, when they encounter new life challenges or feel the stress and anxiety of preparation for a new step in their personal development, they feel suddenly vulnerable. Some return to their habit or dependency to avoid the anxiety. This requires finding ways to handle both the situation and the damaged relationships that it usually creates.

In a Twelve-Step program, Steps Ten, Eleven, and Twelve are relapse prevention steps. While each focuses on a different strategy, together they form a powerful approach to maintaining recovery.

Step Ten restates the need for honesty and responsibility. Cover-ups build upon one another, creating a powerful mesh which traps us in a life of bondage and deceit. Only ongoing self-assessment, open admission of our behaviors and needs, and responsible action can help us avoid this.

Step Eleven aims at deepening spiritual life. You may find that your recovery work leads you to a search for personal spiritual development. Addictions are often simply poor substitutes for spirituality. By deepening your spiritual life you provide for yourself what your addiction provided for you: something you can rely on that is bigger than yourself and all of your fears and limitations. Through invoking a positive power greater than yourself you are able to manage your life. Church or religion is just one way to accomplish this. Alternatively, personal prayer, meditation, or other personal forms of spiritual expression may give you what you need. Inspirational or philosophical reading may be your way, or you might find someone who can act as a mentor or teacher for you.

Step Twelve provides a culminating, final step in the process, pulling you out of your absorption with yourself. Carrying the message to others, showing them the way toward healthy living, giving them the support they need to take their own steps, may be your best way to prevent relapse. You will be the one who truly gains the most. When you reach out to others you reinforce your own learning, develop a broader perspective, and give new purpose and meaning to your ongoing struggle. The best way to learn is to teach; and the best way to experience the life-changing power of recovery is to be a part of the recovery of another.

How Stress Precipitates Relapse

These three steps are a powerful way to prevent relapse. But all too often, on their own they don't work. The common factor in most relapses is stress. We get ourselves into recovery because we want to be free from the chains of our disease. Once we get free of our dysfunctional cycle, staying free is usually difficult but manageable—till we are hit by stress. When our lives become stressful, when we feel inadequate, maintaining recovery becomes more difficult and we are pressured to return to our old ways.

So, how can you live a full, productive, and satisfying life without experiencing a certain amount of stress? Work is stressful, relationships and families are stressful, and the normal changes brought about by personal development and world changes are stressful. It would be unrealistic and shortsighted to believe that you could or even should lead a stress-free life.

Handling stress constructively must become a priority in recovery. To do so, you must first come to understand

- what stresses you out
- how you react to stress
- how to recognize early signs of a stress reaction
- what you can do to break the stress cycle

The rest of this chapter outlines ways to design a system for beating stress. Think it through by yourself or with someone who can help. Then use these stress-busting strategies with Steps Ten, Eleven, and Twelve to smooth out your life before relapse becomes a real threat. In case you do relapse, it is also important to have a plan. Know who you will call and what steps you will take when you find yourself sliding back into behavior that you know heads for trouble.

Red Flags

When we are under stress, we tend to act out. That's when we do the very things we want to change. Sometimes it feels as if stressful situations "out there" cause our stress reactions. If it were that simple, we could move to a deserted island, camp out, and all our problems would be solved. Unfortunately, not only is that not practical, but it ignores our own input into the stress cycle. What we do in response to stressful situations can make them better or worse. And our own responses can be changed.

One person's challenge can be another person's stress. Whether past experiences or personal traits cause this difference is not important, but it *is* important that you have your own "stress profile" of the things you handle better than most and things you don't. You have your own hot spots, specific situations which trigger stress responses in you. Identifying these hot spots is the first part of developing a stress prevention program.

To assess the way in which stress impacts your life, ask yourself the following questions:

Are you overloaded with work?

Sometimes it seems as if work expands, and bosses are never satisfied. Many of us are perfectionists and lose sight of what to reasonably expect of ourselves in a particular situation. And many of us have demanding lives outside of work.

Do you have overwhelming responsibilities?

Feelings of being overwhelmed by responsibility are common to business executives, professionals, and homemakers. Many of us are continually given new responsibilities by families, employers, and friends. These pressures are diverse and they often conflict with one another.

Do you have trouble detaching?

If you find a particular situation or several situations stressful why can't you let go of it or them? What keeps you there, or keeps you so attached that you let it stress you out? What's the hook?

Sometimes we have special vulnerabilities. For example, Steve in Chapter One had trouble getting along with authority figures. His drinking was a way to challenge them, creating difficulty at work, which in turn became increasingly stressful for him. Sometimes we have something to prove. Pleasing people was Elizabeth's proving ground, and she worked harder than anyone to gain approval.

Sean and Tamiko were "hooked" by situations that they found stressful. And like any investor, when we overinvest in one stressful situation that multiplies our level of stress.

Are you having performance problems?

A major problem with stress is that it affects performance. A major problem with poor performance is that it creates stress. Too much stress lowers concentration, short-circuits motivation, and drains away energy, each of which is essential to our lives.

Are you withdrawing from others?

There's an old proverb: "If you want to avoid stress,

don't get involved with your own life!" That's true, and we know it. So well, in fact, that we do it all the time. When we begin to experience burnout, we tend to do an interesting one-two move. First, we get more tenacious and dig in harder. We get tunnel vision, and grimly plod forward, instead of sitting back and figuring out what's wrong. The second thing we do is become numb. We withdraw emotionally from the situation and ice over. In doing so we tend to withdraw from others who might help us think it through and gain perspective. We may even dehumanize others in the situation (like family, friends, or those critical to our work), and treat them like obstacles or objects.

Do you experience role strain?
Life in the fast lane isn't all that easy! Everyone seems to want all of your time and attention. You are expected to fix everyone else's problems. If you wear many hats, you are expected to be a worker at work, a jock on the field, a parent at home, a citizen in public. The expectations others have for you are often unclear, mixed, and even contradictory. Role strain is the stress caused by having contradictory demands placed upon you by others, or by ourself.

Tamiko experienced serious role strain when she felt her parents expected her to keep their traditions and also be a successful career professional. She wasn't able to say no directly, so she sought perfection and control through anorexia.

Are you experiencing decreased satisfaction?
Unhappiness is the bottom line result of these stress reactions. We do the things we do in this world to get happy. When we experience work overload, being over-

whelmed by responsibilities, an inability to detach, over-involvement, performance problems, withdrawal, and role strain, we are not getting satisfaction out of our lives.

As we have seen so far, the signs of stress affect our lives deeply, gradually turning them into unsatisfactory grinds. As one overachieving executive put it, "Hey, it just wasn't fun anymore." And as our unhappiness increases, our resistance to relapse decreases.

Beating the Stress Cycle

The stress cycle begins the moment we enter a potentially stressful situation. What we expect and how we interpret the situation directly affects our emotional reaction to it. This in turn determines how we respond, which in turn makes the situation better or worse. We can start managing stress at one of several points along this cycle.

Adjust your expectations

Here are three ways your expectations can directly influence the stress level of any situation. First, your expectations of the situation itself shape the way you respond to it. When you expect a negative result, you act differently than when you expect a positive result. You often convey a negative attitude, act in negative or defensive ways, and give up trying to work constructively. This has a predictable effect: it is called a "self-fulfilling prophecy." Because you expect it, you help create it.

If you were to let yourself believe that a positive outcome were not only possible but likely, you would convey a more positive attitude, act in positive ways, and work constructively to bring about that result. Because you expected it, you would help create it. Experiment with this the next time a difficult situation arises.

The second way your expectations can influence the situation is the performance you expect from yourself. It is likely that you are pretty hard on yourself. You probably don't really have a limit to what you feel you should do. If you think you could score a ten, and do so, you probably sit around afterwards beating yourself for not getting an eleven. Ease up, and be content with what you do.

The third way expectations complicate the situation is how you expect yourself to cope. When you mentally review a difficult situation, you often persecute yourself twice. First on the basis of your performance, and then again about whether or not you let it bother you. If you feel stress, you blame yourself and make the situation still worse.

Become aware of what goes on in your mind during times of stress. What you expect of the situation, your performance, and your reactions all heavily influence the stress you experience. You may find that a little self-correction can magically turn mountains into molehills.

Deal with your feelings

Once we have been caught up in a situation we expect to be difficult and we interpret as negative, we will react emotionally. Part of our learning to break the stress cycle involves learning to handle our emotions. Some people feel that feelings are uncontrollable, but that is simply not the case. We have far more control over what we feel than most of us care to admit.

Feelings like anger or fear are a little bit like pain. They alert you to the fact that something is wrong. Yet unlike pain, we tend to worship anger or fear. We think of them as an overfilled reservoir that must be drained to avoid damage. Thus we believe that we must

- talk it out
- vent our frustration
- blow off steam
- cry
- explode

Yet research on emotions does not support this. Studies suggest that venting anger tends to produce more anger. "Talking it out" tends to keep people emotionally aroused. Further, high blood pressure, which medical professionals used to feel was connected to "keeping feelings in," is really connected to age, race, social class, and to the cause of the anger.

This does not mean that you shouldn't express your feelings. Getting in touch with how you really feel is an important part in deciding how to handle any situation. It just means that expressing the feelings doesn't solve anything. This also means that when you get frustrated, angry, hurt, or sad, you should not just sit around raging or weeping. Getting stuck in the feelings is a sure way to lose control of the situation.

The only thing that really provides a healthy expression of feelings is using that energy to *change* whatever it was causing the feelings in the first place. Treating anger or fear or sadness as if they were the problem is to misunderstand a natural process. It is like taking an aspirin to reduce the pain when your shoe is too small. You should view emotions as symptoms.

Sometimes we find ourselves unable to take positive

action because our feelings have gotten out of hand. At that point we need some strategies to manage our feelings until we can get back into control. Here are twelve ways:

1. Admit to yourself how you feel.
2. Decide where and when you could better express those feelings, and promise yourself that you will. Follow through.
3. If you have time, take a break and get away from the situation for a while.
4. Talk to someone not connected with the situation; gain perspective.
5. Do some deep breathing or relaxation exercises.
6. Use positive self-messages.
7. Write out what you see happening. Try to work out a plan on paper.
8. Try to figure out what you are really afraid of in the situation and how you can better take care of yourself.
9. Try acting as if you were feeling differently. "Fake it until you make it."
10. Listen to the voice of your body.
11. Create an image of good outcome for the situation. Focus on that image.
12. Think about what kind of help you need and how to get it.

Take effective action

The bottom line in stress busting is whether or not we make the situation worse. Coping strategies may have short-range success but long-range problems. We need to find new solutions to problem situations. An example is alcohol. When we drink, we change our mood and relax. Things seem better. This makes the tension and uncertainty less bothersome. But down the road we pay. We may suffer a hangover, become addicted, or blow it socially. More importantly, we never learn to handle the situation in the first place and so face the same uncomfortable situations again and again.

Think about the major problem situations in your life. What sort of things did you do to cope with them? Looking back on those situations, how effective was your response? Did you make the situation better in the long run or worse? Here are some approaches to positive action:

Stop, take a breath, and ask yourself the following questions about each type of problem situations you regularly face:

- What is going wrong in this situation?
- What is the worst possible outcome for me?
- What is the more likely outcome?
- What am I doing to make the problem worse?
- What would I like to have happen?
- What specific steps could I take to make that happen?

Get some help:

- Find out who might be helpful
- Find out who has dealt successfully with this problem before
- Talk to them

Plan your attack:

- Consider some alternatives
- Decide what you want to do
- Break it down into steps
- Rehearse
- Take first things first
- Focus on one thing at a time

Check the results:

- Make spot checks midway through
- Treat it like an experiment
- Rethink and regroup

Now look at your situations again. Think about how you might handle them differently. What could you have done then or in the future to make it turn around? Take the next problem situation and work it through following these specific steps. Check out the results for yourself.

Some additional strategies for stress management have proven useful for specific situations:

1. If you are having difficulty with expectations, get someone to help. Often it helps to talk to someone

who knows you, to gain perspective on what is and isn't important. This person might also help you sort out what is reasonable to expect of yourself given your differing goals. If the situation is on the job, consider someone who knows your organization and role, but who is neither your supervisor or subordinate. If the situation is in the family, consider finding someone who knows your family well, but is not a part of it.

2. You might try sitting down and clarifying your responsibilities with those people to whom you feel you owe something. Find out just what they expect. Be open to opportunities for negotiating a more reasonable set of expectations.

3. Get clear with yourself what expectations you could more comfortably live with. For each of those, write down a compromise expectation.

4. There are several things you can do about handling overwhelming responsibilities. First, look at the way you prioritize your work or family time. Use the system for each of the responsibilities you feel saddled with. Now, are each of the responsibilities of equal importance? Which ones are less important and don't deserve as much energy? Give time and energy to meeting each responsibility accordingly.

5. If you are having difficulty detaching, perhaps you could take a little time off and spend it with other, less stressful things, which could enrich your life and recharge your batteries. Schedule time for them. See friends or relatives who are not connected with the stressful situation. Make time to

meet your other obligations. Find a way to get some rest and relaxation.

6. If you are baffled by a problem situation, try listing the chain of events leading up to that situation. List the events, stressful conditions, and performance problems you are experiencing. Look for patterns, whatever it is that "hooks" you, and recurring personalities. When you have things sorted out, call in someone you trust to help you solve problems.

7. Consider talking to someone else about your role responsibilities. They might have some suggestions about other ways of looking at them. Similarly, find someone to talk to about the pressures you feel, someone who could simply provide you emotional support.

Finally, in case you still haven't found just the right stress management strategies that would work for you, here are thirty-four more!

be yourself
share more
get more variety in your life
cut the criticism
visualize attractive futures
don't put things off
set yourself up for enjoyment
change your pace
do some good things for others
take naps
meet some new people
let go

exercise your spirituality
focus on your goals
turn it over to a Higher Power
start a journal
pursue a new interest
meditate
give yourself good rewards
get some exercise
take care of your health
sleep regularly and enough
set limits for yourself
play
make necessary changes
consider alternatives
gain an attitude of gratitude
see a counselor
pay attention to your dreams
find a sanctuary
don't do things that hurt you
face fears
surround yourself with good friends

Designing a Relapse Prevention Plan

When we perceive and interpret a situation as threatening, our nervous system starts a complex arousal process. This arousal leads to emergency behavior and further emotional upset. Sometimes this is life-saving, but usually it gets us into trouble. Temporary stress frequently triggers emergency behavior and relapses into habitual problems. The key to dealing with such overwhelming reactions is early awareness. This buys us time to change thought patterns, to take action, to change the situation, to work at handling the feelings, or to change the response itself. Having a plan is essential. If you can gain control over the stress response, you will gain the upper hand in the battle to keep yourself in recovery.

Look back over your answers to the questions in the last section. Use them to design your own plan to prevent relapse by answering the following questions:

- What sorts of situations have proven particularly stressful in the past or do you anticipate to be stressful in the future?

- What steps have you learned to take to manage those situations?

- What sort of personal reactions have you found to indicate that you are too stressed?

- Are there other signs to look for, which indicate that you are at risk of relapse?

- Consider the answers to the previous stress questions, plus the following dysfunctional means of coping with stress. Do you still do any of these:

  minimizing risk
  being ungrateful
  covering up
  lying
  being depressed or full of anxiety
  being drawn to temptation
  lacking faith
  having performance problems
  visiting old haunts
  failure of will
  rejecting advice given by people in recovery

being preoccupied with thoughts of the problem behavior

spending more time with friends who share the problem

- ♦ List the signs that you know will be indications that you are at risk.
- ♦ What steps can you take when you recognize that you are becoming at risk?
- ♦ What will you do if you actually relapse?

In designing an action plan for relapse, first stop and remember what you initially did to break your addiction. It obviously worked, so start there. If you attended meetings, begin again. If you saw a therapist, reschedule a visit. If certain people were particularly supportive and helpful to you, look them up. If you followed a program from a book, dust it off again. Whatever worked the first time met a need that may be again going unmet.

Bear in mind that you may be changing again. Just as Steve's urge to relapse was really a sign that he was ready to move ahead in his personal development, your relapse urges may be a signal of your own readiness for new challenges. You may be ready to come to grips with forgotten parts of your past, new aspects of the present, or even the future. Getting clear on the origin of your distress helps you determine what to do to relieve it.

As you make plans for dealing with urges to relapse, review all of the activities and suggestions you have considered in prior chapters to answer the question, "What shall I do now?"

List the activities you will try and the people you will contact when the urge to relapse becomes strong.

If you have relapsed, or even if the urge to relapse has been difficult, you may have offended or harmed others. Review the exercises from the chapter on making amends; list the ways you will make amends to those you harm.

Relapse is not failure. It is merely a setback during recovery. It is neither cause for giving up nor cause for shame. Facing overwhelming temptation tries your very soul. When such temptation strikes at short range, a contingency plan is essential. Once the immediate temptation is weathered, however you must ask yourself, "Why was the temptation so great?" Relapse is a sign that things have become unbalanced again. Relapse signals a time for reassessment, revitalization of your recovery plan, and recommitment to your future.

♦ ♦ ♦

Brenda, *a crack addict, hasn't used for eight months. Although she has stopped frequenting nightclubs and hanging out with her friends who use, she is still feeling compulsive.*

Brenda's days were busy. Work took up most of her daytime and she would read or go out in the evenings. She would see a couple of new friends now and then, yet time seemed to drag.

Sometimes Brenda would start to get desperate again. It would start quietly enough with a little boredom, some feelings of loneliness. Attempting to avoid the discomfort, she would ignore her feelings and look for entertainment. Then she would "forget" to call her sponsor Carrie or her friends, get angry at people, and blame her job for not being just right.

At this point Brenda would start thinking about the bar down the street. Even though she didn't drink very much, she was tempted to go in to see what was happening. Perhaps she could meet someone interesting.

During these periods she would have trouble with people at work. She would start backsliding into her old ways of stirring up trouble and would get snippy with customers. Usually she caught herself in time to make the necessary apologies and she would get angry at herself for doing it.

Her journal proved to be helpful. In it she could write about the events of the day, things that had happened long ago, and even her hopes and dreams for the future. Sometimes she would have different people talk to one another, or have herself saying things to them which she could never do in real life.

One evening she had written:

> In my dream last night I was walking in the spring rain. I had come out of a dark forest into a beautiful meadow that stretched upwards to the foot of a high mountain. The mountain was covered with clouds, but I knew it was there, and I could hear streams rushing from glacier meltwater. Pink, yellow, and purple flowers pushed up from the long deep green grass, blooming in the light rain. The path I followed meandered upwards toward a waterfall and the peak beyond. As I paused for breath and looked up, the swirling clouds parted long enough to give me a glimpse of the stunning snow covered mountain peak against a brilliant blue sky.
>
> I feel as if I am on the right path. I think that I am going in the right direction. If only I can stay on the path and not lose my nerve or get lost following some false trail.

The dream haunted her. She knew it meant that her recovery was close at hand, even when she was feeling down. Her life was full of possibility even though there were perils. She also knew recovery was a day-to-day proposition.

Tonight, instead of giving in to the uneasy feelings she

chose to write in her journal again. It had become less of a report on what she had been experiencing and more of a process of problem-solving on paper. She found herself changing as she wrote. Brenda made the following entry:

> I'm going crazy looking at this room. I keep thinking about going down to the bar, but I know that's a bad idea. I think the long evenings are the worst. Don was talking about the financial management courses through University Extension. They have a certificate course, which starts next week. If I finished that by next year, I could be opening up some different career options. Maybe I'll do it.
>
> I'm still wondering what Carrie meant when she said she got more out of helping me than I got. How could she, when I got so much?

Brenda put on her coat and went for a walk. At the sidewalk, she turned the opposite direction from the bar and proceeded uptown. As she walked she thought more about Carrie's befriending her. How could Carrie get something of value out of listening to her make mistakes and agonize over situations which could obviously be changed? What could she, Brenda, get from listening to someone else?

Before she realized it, Brenda found herself near the community center where her NarcAnon meetings were held. She realized it had been some time since she had attended a meeting, and that one was now in progress. She considered going in, but hesitated. It seemed like such an effort and she had been doing so well. It wasn't that clear how going over the same material again could help her now, yet something inside told her that she should.

As she stood in front of the building wrestling with the decision, she became aware of someone sitting on a bench in the dark. Whoever it was sniffled quietly and Brenda realized that she was crying.

Brenda went over. "Excuse me. Are you OK?"
"Yes," the girl hesitated. "No, I don't know."
"Are you waiting for someone?"
"Not really."

Brenda wondered if the girl was planning to go into the meeting. "Listen," she said, sitting down, "my name is Brenda. Are you sure there isn't anything I can help with?"

The girl looked at her in the dark. "I don't know. I came here to go to a meeting. It's in there." She glanced at the center doors. "Now I'm not so sure. My name is Maria."

"Maria, did you hear about the meeting from someone?" Brenda thought that it might help her understand why Maria had come.

"A friend told me it might help. I'm kind of mixed up right now."

Brenda thought of Carrie. "I'm going in," she offered. "If you need some moral support, we could go together."

Part II

Healing the Past Within Us

The next step after recovery consists of exploring why we went astray, and healing the early childhood experiences that led to the compulsive or addictive behavior.

In this part we address various forms of past hurt and constructive ways you can confront, integrate, and move beyond them. Chapter Five deals with victimization issues, and presents a method of reliving the trauma through writing in order to release unexpressed feelings and reach out to others. Chapter Six looks at unresolved grief, showing how that grief can limit our lives, and pointing the way toward resolution. Chapter Seven explores the difficulties of disturbed family relationships and presents strategies for healthy ways to cope with and correct family problems. You can learn a great deal from all of these chapters, but make sure to spend time with the one that addresses your particular situation. If you are to move beyond stabilization to fuller growth and richer personal fulfillment, resolving your early trauma is critical.

One of the most powerful ways we can relive and release our pain is through writing. Thus the three chapters in this part utilize extensive writing exercises. These allow you to explore areas of discomfort privately, at your own pace.

Even so, this can be a difficult task. It can call up painful and frightening memories. Sometimes these memories are overwhelming in intensity and cause distress, particularly if your familiar coping strategies such as alcohol, drugs, and food are no longer available.

For this reason finding support is critical. Try to get several people to agree to be listeners, people who you can talk with about the exercises, your experiences, and your reactions. Choose someone you can trust with sensitive or potentially embarrassing information—someone who will not use the information against you, or attempt to act in your behalf.

It is very important to know how to contact a mental health professional, in case your reactions are more serious than you anticipated. Dealing with the past can be stressful. Find ways to take good care of yourself while you work on your past hurts. Don't make big decisions, don't take on extra work, and *don't* act quickly without thinking it through. Get enough rest, eat well, exercise, and make sure you have time alone to think. Keep a journal of your personal reactions and discoveries during this very important time.

When you deal with painful memories, watch out for:

- problems concentrating, flashbacks, disorientation, fears of "losing your mind"
- difficulty coping with ordinary life tasks
- waves of uncontrollable emotions such as fear, sadness, despair, or hysteria

- unfocused agitation, or ritualistic or uncontrolled behavior
- inability to care for yourself or your children
- thoughts about violence or ending your own life

If you experience any of these, see a mental health professional as soon as possible.

5

Letting Go of Past Hurt

If you have been victimized by traumatic incidents in your life, this chapter will help you work through painful memories. It will help you understand the way in which trauma helped lead you to your compulsion or addiction and how it works to maintain it as well.

To understand our own past hurts we must understand how our experiences have affected us. As we mature, our world expands. We soak up facts and truths about the world like sharks in a feeding frenzy. We digest this new information by placing it in our internal world view, and work hard at integrating it with the things we have learned previously. We struggle to understand things in a way in that makes sense of our world and our lives.

To make sense, our world must be orderly and not chaotic. This allows us to trust it enough to risk ourselves in the process of growing and changing. If we can't trust the world to be orderly, we cannot believe that our life efforts will pay off. If we can't trust the world, we can't change and grow. We can't risk loving others or investing in future goals.

Some experiences are so frightening and overwhelming that they call into question our view of an orderly world. As a result of major accidents, abuse, or other kinds of victimization, we learn to experience the world as cruel and capricious, and we lose our trust that it will support and nurture us. We can no longer approach the world with a basic optimism, an "existential faith," and trust that it is, on the whole, a safe place. We become so afraid of the potential hurt others may cause that our attachments bring us pain, and we avoid them.

Thus, as a result of being traumatized, we may learn to live by the following rules:

- Don't believe
- Don't trust
- Don't care
- Don't invest
- Don't love yourself

Some traumas, such as incest or physical abuse, happen over an extended period of time. In our efforts to survive the situation, we may have adopted coping strategies such as:

- narrowing our awareness to include only what is important to survive
- becoming vigilant and suspicious of everything
- becoming emotionally detached
- becoming stubbornly determined just to "get through"
- suspending our belief in ourself, our judgments, and our abilities

These emergency coping systems usually work, and we do get through. Because they work, and because of the tremendous stress caused by natural reactions to our world coming apart, we tend to maintain these coping systems. Later, they become lifestyles.

Long after the traumatic events are over, these reactions persist. Our further development may be hindered by our constricted, survival-based world view. Many problems such as substance abuse, codependent relationships, and compulsive disorders develop from attempts to cope with long-term reactions to early traumas.

In order to recover from the traumatic experience, we must dismantle these coping systems. Healing requires us to regain our unity with the world by:

- overcoming the anxieties and fears we learned from being victimized
- letting go of things and people whose loss we cannot accept
- learning how our early family experiences shaped our current expectations regarding relationships
- rebuilding a more realistic way of looking at the world, one that allows options and growth
- reestablishing trust that the world will meet our needs
- reattaching to people, things, and conditions
- recapturing a sense of meaning, purpose, and direction
- learning to accept and love ourselves again

The first step in overcoming the self-limitations of our coping systems is to open ourselves to the pain we have been avoiding. We must relive the hurtful experiences so that we can release the life energy which has been blocked to protect us from pain. We must open ourselves so that we may recreate our unity with the world.

A great many people have been victimized by assault, rape or abuse, others have been in accidents and natural disasters. Despite the commonality of post-traumatic reactions, people who have been traumatized often isolate themselves and feel alone in their pain. Their first need is to learn to reach out. To overcome isolation you must let others know when you are in pain. This can be hard, but it can also amount to a breakthrough in healing.

◆ ◆ ◆

Carmen *is a relationship addict who has trouble with intimacy. She has been married twice, but each marriage ended when she became pregnant and chose to have an abortion.*

A night breeze rustled the leaves outside Carmen's study. Although it was after midnight, she sat at her desk reading the workbook she'd found in the bookstore. As it had instructed, she had several pens and some extra paper standing ready. She felt apprehensive.

And well she should. She had been avoiding this moment for nearly twenty-five years. At the time she was molested there had been only fear. Her stepfather (she still couldn't bring herself to think his name) had threatened her into silence. Later she was paralyzed by shame. She felt responsible for what had occurred and responsible for protecting her mother's feelings. Still later, she feared being kicked out of her mother's life as she rocked the boat, and being rejected by the kids at school if they ever found out.

During the past several years Carmen had turned her back on the whole business as she went about shaping her new life. It had been a long time, and it simply seemed easier to ignore the whole thing, as if it were a bad dream. The memories were too painful.

But she could not deny the effects the experience had on her adult life. She had great difficulty trusting men and, while she had been married, she had always protected herself emotionally. While she looked toward relationships for love and affection, she always avoided real intimacy. Carmen knew this was a problem, but she couldn't release the fear. Only now was she beginning to sense some sort of connection between her running away from the memories and her problems with relationships.

Do I really want to go through with this? she thought. Am I setting myself up for more hurt? Wouldn't it be easier to close this thing right now and walk away? The breeze stirred the leaves outside her window again. Carmen opened the book.

With resolve matched only by the uncertainty she felt, Carmen wrote her name in the space provided. There, she thought, I have begun.

As she worked through the sections, the questions became more difficult. She was asked to describe her abuse, focusing on one incident. The fleeting images she had were disturbing, and when she tried to put them into words she went blank. She tried to calm herself by having a snack and going to the bathroom. Then she started again.

She remembered the first time she had heard him enter the room in the dark. She could tell it was him because his breath smelled of alcohol. He hadn't said much. She remembered how rough his hands were, she remembered his weight, and how uncomfortable and confused she was, but not much more. Later, he had said, "This is our secret. If you tell your mother, it will hurt her a lot. She won't love you anymore, and you will have to go live in a foster home."

Following the book's directions, Carmen wrote down just what she had seen. That was easy, because it had been dark. Vague shapes and shadows. She remembered watching the street light shining through the window and patterning the bedspread. Then she remembered seeing him on the bed, naked. That memory made her shudder.

Next Carmen focused upon sounds. She could hear the "click" of the door latch as it opened. She could hear the way he had talked to her. The memory made her stomach churn, and she felt a great sinking feeling. It took her ten minutes to pull her strength together and get back to writing.

She tried to remember the physical sensations, but these were harder. She remembered the roughness of his hands. Funny, she thought, no emotional reaction. She recalled his pressing weight upon her. Sitting at her desk, Carmen had trouble breathing. As she wrote about the feeling of being pressed down, she found herself taking sudden deep breaths, as if to reassure herself that she could still breathe. I wonder, she thought, if that has anything to do with the fact that I have never really enjoyed sex, even in my marriages. Or especially in my marriages.

The writing became easier. Remembered sensations became images, images turned to words, words led to sentences. After a while Carmen looked up. She had been writing nonstop for over an hour.

As she wrote she felt herself coming nearer and nearer to understanding something. It wasn't so much the physical pain. Not even the feeling of being intimidated, controlled, and used. The abuse had been bad, but there was something much worse, which had pulled the rug right out from under her. Finally it came clear. Her stepfather had been awful, but it was her mother who had hurt her the worst. Carmen now had the connection she needed: when she *had* told her mother, her mother had not believed her. She had denied the abuse, and minimized and ignored it. And for a reason: she had not wanted Carmen to come between her and her new husband. She had betrayed her daughter's trust and wellbeing to protect her marriage. Carmen had been sold out.

♦ ♦ ♦

Carmen tossed in her sleep. It was happening all over again. The door latch had clicked, the shadowy figure approached and sat down on her bed. Rough hands gave way to the oppressive weight. Carmen could not breathe. She fought for breath and started to scream. This time she shouted "Stop!"

The dream changed. It was the empty dry lake bed. The deep azure sky was cloudless and the distant mountains shimmered in the heat. She was alone. Carmen turned and saw the long black car. People she knew, including her stepfather, were climbing in to drive away and leave her. This time Carmen was not panicked. She was not terrified of the coming isolation—she was angry. Furiously, she ran to the car, reaching it before the door closed. Yanking it open, she dragged her stepfather out of the car, pummeling him with her fists. He struggled to his feet and started running away across the lake bed. She turned to face her mother....

♦ ♦ ♦

As the early morning light spilled through the window and across the cafe table, Carmen found her feedback friend, Rita, sipping coffee.

"Hi," replied Carmen. "Thanks for meeting me for breakfast at such short notice. I've been up half the night and I need your feedback."

Rita smiled as she sat down. "I figured it was important."

Carmen looked thoughtful. "You know what, Rita? I've

been thinking. I've been crazy for a long time."

"What do you mean?" asked Rita.

"I've been hurt, angry, and frantic for so long, I've forgotten what 'normal' looks like." Rita smiled again. Carmen continued, "I've been running for a long, long time."

"From . . . " prompted Rita.

"From my stepfather, Frank," replied Carmen " . . . and what he did to me. And from my mother. I've been desperately trying to keep from being rejected, and at the same time, I've been keeping people away. I need people, but I don't trust them. I've been paying twenty years for what he did to me, and for my mother not believing me. I've paid enough."

Rita thought for a moment. "What are you going to do? Do you think it's time to see a therapist?"

"This is a start," said Carmen, pushing an envelope across the table. It contains all of the things I have wanted to say to Frank for all those years. I confront him with what he did and what it meant to me. I demand an apology and I tell him what I want from him. I'm going to write one to my mother next. Would you read it?"

Rita opened the letter. "Dear Frank," it began.

◆ ◆ ◆

Just as Carmen discovered, anyone who has experienced past hurt faces two choices. One alternative is to attempt to ignore or live with the hurt. But this isn't possible without sacrificing the future. The cost of silence is great: self-hatred, isolation, the development of a compulsion or addiction, and a lifestyle that precludes growth. The other alternative is to confront the hurt and work to heal it. This is better, but it is neither comfortable nor easy.

We begin the healing process by going public, retelling the story of our hurt in its fullness. In order to protect ourselves from pain we had created an incomplete, partial picture of the hurtful incident—one we could tolerate and live with, despite inaccuracies and distortions. It allowed us to go on with our lives at the time, but now creates a problem. By keeping us from owning up to deeper feelings and understanding the event in its wholeness, our self-protective fiction keeps the traumatic feelings alive and keeps us from living fully in the present. In order to let go of our fears, pain, and protective lifestyles, we must fill out and complete that story. The central process includes preparing ourselves for retelling the story, reliving the incident, releasing the feelings, filling out a more complete version of the incident, and sharing the full story with others.

Everyone has a story. A story about what happened to them, and, for better or worse, how it shaped who they are and what they do. Most people have experienced at least one very difficult experience such as the divorce of their parents, the death or suicide of someone close, or an accident, rape, or assault. Many have experienced several, or even a whole series of traumatic events. These experiences taught us negative things about ourselves and the world. They lead us to the sort of destructive activities and patterns from which we are now trying to recover.

Telling Your Story

An excellent way to proceed with retelling is to embark upon a writing project. If you don't already have one, get a notebook and keep notes as you read, think about, and experience the rest of this chapter. At the end you can go back and consolidate your notes into a complete written story.

Telling your story will challenge you to enter into a dialogue with yourself and deal with your past in ways you may have never dreamed possible. You should take several steps in order to get the most out of the process.

- **Prepare yourself properly.** This task will not be easy, and it cannot be done by someone else. You must find a method that works for you, whether it involves joining a group, prayer or meditation, service to others, or writing. You must prepare yourself for the pain involved in your healing.
- **Relive the incident.** Allow your memories in. Recapture and relive as much of the memory "data" as you can. You must reexperience the incident and recollect your reactions as completely as possible.
- **Release the feelings.** You must become aware of your deep feelings about the incident, about others who were involved, and about yourself. You must begin expressing those feelings to yourself and to others. Only then will you be able to release those feelings and free yourself.
- **Complete the story.** Your partial, distorted version of the incident must be completed in full form. This completed story, if true to your experience, combines the intensity of the moment with the perspective of the following years. It is an expression of a very important part of you. It is your story, and a part of who you really are.
- **Go public.** You must share your story with others. Tell them what you have been through and its importance to you now.

At each stage of your crisis you experienced a barrage of sensations, impressions, reactions, and interpretations. What you experienced and what you may recall, however, are two different things. Usually, all that you remember is the main focus of the experience. Yet this may be only a partial version of the crisis. You were probably struggling at the time to keep order and avoid harm. In emergencies, the mind tends to simplify and attend to only what is necessary for survival. Much important information gets ignored. Later, when safe, you try and reconstruct what happened. There is more data available, which can give you different perspectives and help you to make more sense of the experience.

In the process of writing your story you will explore each stage of your crisis. In some of the sections below you will answer general questions about your experience. In others, you will recall specific sensory memories. Some may be easy, some quite difficult. You will probably find all of them interesting. Begin the process of thinking and writing about your experiences by first looking at the setting in which it occurred.

Setting the Stage

What background factors set the stage for your crisis? What did you bring to the incident that allowed it to become critical for you?

Let's explore some of the possible elements. Several things could have set you up for your reaction to this incident. Perhaps you were sensitized to this type of incident through early family conditioning or events. Earlier traumas or other learning experiences could have left you particularly vulnerable. If the crisis occurred within the context of work, school, church, or an other organization, there might have been issues and pressures that made it especially difficult for you. Similarly, you may have been experiencing pressures from home or work that had the cumulative effect of stressing you out before the crisis even began. Finally, you might have had unrealistic expectations that caused you to evaluate your own behavior and reactions too harshly.

Think about each of the following background factors carefully. Write down which factors you feel might have compounded your situation. Use short phrases, sentences, or even brief paragraphs if possible.

1. **Were there family themes or issues involved in this incident?** Think about early family experiences and relationships. Did any family emergencies that resemble this experience occur? In reviewing memory fragments, can you recall incidents, anecdotes, or even family legends or stories that might relate to the crisis?

2. **Did the type of incident have some particular meaning to you personally?** Did it play upon or challenge aspects of you that you don't feel good about? Did old themes of personal inadequacy or personal character flaws arise? Were old wounds reopened? If this incident involved loss, had you suffered terrible loss before? If this incident involved victimization, had you been victimized before?

3. If the crisis occurred at work, at church, or within some other organization to which you belong, **were there organizational pressures going on at the time?** Did the crisis point out some critical

flaw in the life of the organization which has been difficult for you? Were there issues of poor leadership, transition, personal accountability, preexisting problems, or other things that bothered you about the organization and made the crisis worse? Did the crisis stand as a symbol of what was going wrong already? Did the incident itself create a larger crisis within the organization?

4. **What was your level of stress at the time of the incident?** Did you go into the situation stressed out already? What was going on at home or at work that could have set you up for your reaction to the crisis? Had you been going through difficult personal changes? Were there any losses, transitions, or new responsibilities that had you stretched out thin already?

5. Prior to the crisis, **what were your expectations regarding the sort of situation in which the crisis occurred?** Were you expecting anything of this sort to happen? What were your expectations of your own performance? Prior to the incident, did you think that you would have handled this sort of incident calmly, effectively, and without repercussions? Or did you expect to fall apart, be unable to cope, and mishandle things?

Any and all of these background factors can set the stage for your particular response to the incident. If you feel that you did not handle it well, or that it should not have affected you in the way it did, you might reevaluate yourself in light of these factors. It may be that your reaction was less an indication of who you were than simply a reflection of what was going on in your life at the time.

If you have been beating yourself up over it, perhaps it's time to lighten up!

Recalling the Event

Sights, sounds, smells, tastes, touches, body sensations, and feelings are the building blocks of memories. Each moment of a crisis is accompanied by those sensations, and each sensory memory combines with others to complete the memory of that step. To adequately tell the story of your traumatic experience, you must start by gathering the individual sensory data and then combining it. Begin by compiling sensory memories in your notebook. Then you can add new recollections as they emerge.

If this event was traumatic for you, it was probably emotionally overwhelming and full recall may be difficult. Before beginning, it might be a good idea to take some precautions.

1. Give yourself plenty of time. Once started, you will want to take as long as necessary to get what you came for.

2. Provide for privacy, so you can become absorbed without interruption.

3. Have a support person available in case you need him or her. This could be a loved one, a trusted friend, or a professional.

4. Consider debriefing with someone afterward, to share the memories, feelings, and things you have learned. Talking is an excellent way to sort through all the things that come up.

5. Plan to exercise and burn off your body's chemical response to the powerful sensory stimulus your memories will provide. This will relieve some of your stress.

6. Plan a reward. Be good to yourself. Buy something nice or treat yourself to an uplifting show. See someone special or go somewhere that feels good. Whatever you consider a reward, do it. You will have certainly earned it!

Sights

As you recall the event, first focus only on your visual memories. Start with the most obvious people, actions, and events and describe them in short phrases. Then relax and go through the incident again. Look for details. Can you see things you missed before? Write down details you remember, even if they didn't seem important at the time.

Look at the scene from different perspectives. Look for things you might have missed before. Look for details in the outer edges of your picture. Check out colors, textures, actions, and faces for new meanings. Imagine looking at yourself at the time, and notice how you looked. Float over the situation, looking at it from above.

Sounds

Take the same approach with the sounds you remember. Relax, set up the situation visually, and then include the sounds. Begin to focus more on the sounds you hear. Separate out different sounds from one another, looking for the significant ones. After you have isolated some sounds, become aware of how those affected you. Listen to them over and over, and feel your deeper response. Pay attention to the impact each of them had and has upon you. This includes background noise, conversations, and other sounds, which you now understand to be important in the situation. When you write down the sounds, try to name each one, describe it, and relate your response to it.

Now go back and write down each sound fragment you recall.

Smells and tastes

Smells and tastes add a dimension of realism and intensity to memories of the past. Relax again. Recall the sights and sounds of the incident. Then open your memories to the smells and tastes of the moment. When you write them down, try to both name and describe what it is, as well as place it in context.

Touch

During the incident you may have had some sort of physical contact. It may have been as subtle as the feel of your clothing or movements, or as commanding as pain. You may have been injured. You may have touched or been touched in ways that impacted you. Relive the event again, focusing upon touch (skin sensation) or body sensations (deep tissue feelings, movement, or physical reaction). Relate memories of skin touch and bodily sensations such as pressure, visceral sensations, or physical action. Write down each in terms of what happened and how it felt.

Feelings

Often we find it very difficult to remember the things we

felt in a crisis situation. Usually we feel a lot, and often more than we can easily recall. Many times we remember only one predominant feeling, to the exclusion of several other, perhaps conflicting feelings. Our mind helps us survive the crisis by automatically going into tunnel vision, but the feelings and "unimportant" details remain with us.

When detailing your feelings, it may be helpful to have some reminders. Below is a list of 120 frequently experienced feelings; they tend to focus on negative emotions, or emotions more likely to arise in crisis.

alert	excited	alive	sensitive
strong	good	anticipating	amused
capable	happy	sure	untroubled
secure	determined	concerned	appreciated
respected	empathetic	elated	enthusiastic
daring	smart	courageous	suspicious
disgusted	resentful	bitter	fed-up
spiteful	listless	moody	full of hatred
lethargic	gloomy	dismal	discontented
tired	dejected	unhappy	bored
bad	forlorn	weary	disappointed
frustrated	sad	depressed	sick
disconsolate	dissatisfied	fatigued	angry
hurt	miserable	pained	lonely
cynical	exhausted	indifferent	unsure
impatient	dependent	unimportant	regretful
torn-up	inadequate	ineffectual	helpless
resigned	apathetic	shamed	worn-out
useless	weak	hopeless	forlorn
rejected	guilty	worthless	impotent
futile	abandoned	estranged	degraded
puzzled	edgy	upset	reluctant
timid	mixed-up	baffled	nervous

tempted	tense	worried	troubled
frightened	anxious	dismayed	apprehensive
panicky	disturbed	shocked	full of dread
trapped	horrified	afraid	scared
terrified	threatened	sullen	provoked
disdainful	alarmed	annoyed	contemptuous
antagonistic	vengeful	indignant	mad

Try reexperiencing the sights and sounds again—close your eyes and recreate the situation in your mind. Look around and notice more details. Focus more upon your own reactions. Then go over the list and look for each feeling in your recreated scene.

Now write down your feelings, putting short phrases wherever possible (e.g., instead of "anxious" it may be more complete to say "increasingly anxious" or "more and more anxious as time went on"). You may need several attempts, or even several writing sessions to get complete. Modify and revise the list continually, as new memories emerge.

Your reactions

Some responses to critical incidents are quite normal. They are universal psychological, emotional, physical, and behavioral signs of stress reactions to emergencies. The list on page 101 may help you recall your response to the full impact stage of your incident. Go through the list and circle those reactions you experienced at the time.

If your experience feels complete, fine! But remain open to new memories, details, nuances, or perspectives that may come in trickles or bursts during the day or at night.

If your experience feels incomplete, that's all right,

Thoughts	Physical Reactions
confusion	sweating
time distortions	pale or flushed skin
impaired thinking	fainting
mental slowness	headaches
thoughts out of control	nausea/vomiting
problems prioritizing	staring, dull eyes
problems making decisions	

Feelings	Behaviors
fear	irritability
anxiety, clinging	hyperactivity (too fast)
explosive anger	hypoactivity (too slow)
intolerable frustration	aimless wandering
unusual lack of reaction	lack of control
detachment	

too. It is all part of the process. You may wish to return several times to repeat the exercise, and if you do, you will probably get more each time. Give yourself time.

If you have uncovered things you can't cope with, or if this approach simply is not working for you, then consider seeing a professional for help. Get someone who is experienced with trauma, and someone you can trust. Be gentle with yourself.

Aftershocks

After the crisis resolved and after the dust had settled, was it really over for you? For some, the end of the crisis is only the beginning of the pain; the full impact of the event is not felt until later. Sometimes days or weeks, sometimes months or years go by before the most troublesome reactions to crisis surface. And sometimes traumas leave scars that seem permanent.

In this section you will explore some of the delayed reactions you may have had. First, consider the external changes in your life caused by the event. Then think about some of the internal changes. Finally, assess whether those internal changes developed into lasting problems.

Changes outside

A crisis upsets the things that structure our lives. We depend upon things such as pace and routine for our sense of security and belonging. We count on them to make our achievements, our values, and the realization of our dreams possible. Crises often strike this structure directly, and alter our lives.

When responding to the following questions about external changes, take your time and think about each one carefully. Note your answers in full sentences or paragraphs, giving as much detail as possible. Try to indicate what each change meant to you, how you felt about it then, and how you feel about it now.

- How were your physical condition and capabilities changed by the incident?
- Was your family changed? How so?
- Were your social relationships and close friends affected?
- How were your standard of living and physical security changed?

- Were special places and locations that had important meaning to you altered or destroyed?
- Were your future options affected by the crisis?
- How has your present situation been shaped by that incident?

Changes within

Changes outside of ourselves hurt us and bring about changes within. We may lose our bearings and our sense of direction. Our lives may be derailed for a while in ways we did not anticipate, and we struggle inside to accommodate the changes outside.

Just as our reactions to the emergency itself were complex, our later reactions can be diverse and confusing. They can also be much more intense than we would expect. Sometimes people worry that they are losing their mind because of delayed reactions to the incident. These reactions affect our thought patterns, our feelings, our physical condition, and our behavior.

It might be helpful to look at the chart on the next page for some common delayed reactions to crisis.

Looking over these reactions, you may recognize some of your own. In developing a full account of your experience you will also need to include your delayed reactions, the ones that surface now.

Using the previous list as a reminder, write a sentence or so describing each of your own later experiences. It might be helpful to mention approximately how long after the incident each occurred.

Quite likely many of the later reactions you have written about went away over time. It is also likely some of them didn't, and those that didn't are the very issues

Thoughts

trouble planning
preoccupation with
  incident
orientation toward past
fear of "going crazy"
denial of incident,
  or its importance

Physical Reactions

fatigue
increased illness
physical concerns
psychosomatic illness
weight change

Feelings

depression
grief/loss
fear of reoccurrence

anxieties/panic
inappropriate anger
unusual fears
oversensitivity
inappropriate crying

Behavior

sleep problems/nightmares
social withdrawal
compulsive talking about
  incident
avoidances
family problems
drinking or drugs
rapid lifestyle changes
problems at school
acting out sexually
running away
problems with the police
flashbacks

that led you to this book. Which of these inner changes are still going on? Have they settled into a repetitive cycle that still bothers you? Go back over this list and circle those that are a problem for you.

You might also have been affected in less obvious ways. Because of past hurts, many people are so fearful of further hurt they never take chances, never learn to live.

They may adopt a lifestyle of avoiding relationships, success, and potentially rewarding adventures to protect themselves from any possible chance of further trauma. In what ways have you limited yourself because of the incident?

Other people are affected the opposite way. They seem to be drawn to risky situations or situations resembling the incident in which they were traumatized. Sometimes this is almost like an addiction. Other times it is an attempt to reconstruct the traumatic event so that it can be mastered. In what ways have you made life choices and adopted styles or pursued interests because of the incident?

What to do with your story

By now you probably have a large notebook full of memories, thoughts, reflections, and plans. Now is the time to consolidate those notes into one complete story. Use the following outline and include all the details you have written to flesh it out.

_____'s Story

1. Background and setting
2. Recalling the incident
3. Reactions at the time
4. Delayed reactions
5. Changes in my life
6. What I need to do now
7. What it all means

Some hints about writing your story: don't feel you have to write the finished product the first time through. Just cut up your notes and paste them together in the right order. Illustrate your story with examples whenever possible. Consider adding line drawings, old photographs, memorabilia, or even collages cut from magazines for added realism. Don't worry about being a great writer. Worry only about getting your story told.

Here are some things to do with your story when it is finished:

- Type it (or have it typed) and run off several copies
- Share it with people whom you love and who care for you
- Show it to your therapist, minister, or other professional
- Join a writing group or support group and share it with them
- Think about getting it in print to benefit others
- Tear it up or burn it
- Keep writing!

Unfinished Business

Sometimes traumas leave unfinished business. Carmen needs to say several things to her stepfather. Until she does, she will be unable to leave the trauma in her past. While we may never be able to undo the damage or rewrite history, we may be able to change the way we feel about the incident and about ourselves by taking action.

Unfinished business may be taken care of by

- writing letters
- personal confrontation
- particular actions or symbolic rituals
- visits to the trauma site
- communicating with others who were there
- receiving apologies or amends
- speaking out publicly or taking political action
- sharing your story with others who were there, or have had similar experiences.

Do you have things that you must do before you can put the incident to rest?

You'll probably discover that as time goes on you will find yourself thinking about this more and more. New memories may arise and new connections may occur between what happened long ago and what happens in your life right now. That's good! That's healing. Be open to these revelations and make all the additions and changes to your notes and plans that you want.

In general, the world can hurt us more than we can ever hurt back. But taking action in our own behalf is healing. Although we cannot change the events of our past, we can face them, release ourselves from their pain, and move forward with newfound self-respect and dignity.

6

Working with Loss and Grief

Many people carry a special burden through life—the pain of loss. It is an unseen weight upon their souls, something they are trying to forget. If you have undergone loss in your life, this chapter will help you understand the way in which the loss contributed to your addictive behavior. Many people feel they have not experienced loss in their lives, but once they look deeper, surprise themselves with the losses they really have experienced and the pain that is still alive.

Loss figures heavily in the lives of all addicts and dependents. As a result of their desperate actions, they lose friends, property, respect from others, and even their own identity. In recovering from their compulsions, they also faced other losses, including that which they relied upon for comfort and structure—the addiction itself.

As Margaret discovers, things she has taken for granted in her life have strongly influenced the way in which she deals with her emotions—without her knowing it.

◆ ◆ ◆

***Margaret** is a recovering overeater who is just starting to deal with the early loss of an older sister.*

Margaret sat at the kitchen table reading. The dinner dishes were cleared and Tanya, her daughter, was doing her English homework while Margaret gave moral support.

"Mom, I don't understand this poem at all," complained Tanya. "What does Frost mean by 'miles to go before I sleep'?"

"I think he means that he has much to do before he dies," Margaret explained, barely looking up from her book.

"Well, does he look forward to dying or something?" Tanya persisted.

This time Margaret put her book down and focused on the poem. "Not really, I think it's just that sometimes life seems so overwhelming that death seems like a relief." She looked at Tanya. How much she resembled Margaret's mother. Maybe even Angela, Margaret's sister who had died when she was sixteen. Tanya was now fifteen.

"Hmm." Tanya started to read again, and then stopped. "Have you ever felt that way?"

"Not really. I don't know." That was a hard one for Margaret. "I think life is short enough. I want to be around to enjoy it." She thought about Tanya not living past sixteen and shuddered.

Pretty soon it was time for Tanya to go to bed and Margaret was left alone. She found herself distracted and unable to read. She wanted something, but wasn't sure what. Maybe food would do it. There was some ice cream in the freezer. She found herself staring at the freezer. No way, she thought. I've quit my bingeing.

Tearing herself away, Margaret moved into the family room. Still antsy, she flipped channels on the TV, as if it would provide her with what was missing. What was missing?

She wandered into her study and sat in the semidarkness, determined to see this through without eating. She felt a wave of sadness rush over her. Maybe it had something to do with Tanya's poem. It had been troubling, but she wasn't sure why.

More waves of sadness hit. This was about some sort of loss, she realized, but she could not identify it. No one she knew had died lately, nor was anyone sick. She somehow felt she should let the sadness in instead of fighting it. She let herself feel it, crying softly. It was as if the sadness was an old acquaintance, or someone who had been around a long time. It was familiar, even though she didn't understand it.

She began to notice that when she fought against the sadness, she felt anxious, but when she gave herself over to the sadness, she felt differently. Sometimes she would get angry, sometimes more deeply depressed, and sometimes even strangely comfortable. Also, it wasn't so much the image of dying that brought on the sadness, but the idea of fighting it. This was confusing; of course you should fight death! Life is worth keeping, and dying is frightening, so why would fighting death be a problem for her?

Her memory drifted to the hospital visits many decades ago. She recalled her parents calling her into their bedroom one morning early, telling her that her sister had "passed on." Margaret remembered asking when she would be back. Her mother had left the room, and her father hadn't said much. Later that day her parents had gotten all dressed up and left her with a neighbor. Then they had come back and people had brought over food, and other people came and stood around talking quietly. Her sister's room had remained unchanged for several months until Margaret had been moved into it.

♦ ♦ ♦

"What was her name?" asked her counselor, Dr. Lamont.

"Angela," said Margaret. She felt a little strange saying

her name aloud. Her family hadn't talked about Angela at all after she died.

Dr. Lamont looked at Margaret with one of those "now-think-carefully" looks. "Were you the bearer of Angela's life?"

"What?"

"Sometimes families refuse to deal with their grief. Some keep the deceased's room intact as a shrine, refuse to get rid of clothes, never mention the deceased's name, and even let another family member take over the deceased's role. You said earlier that Angela was the smart one, the one who was to go to college and succeed, while you were the baby. You were allowed to do pretty much what you pleased. Did that change with your sister's death?"

Margaret remembered the first report card she got after Angela's death. Grades had never mattered before. Her father had frowned and said that things were going to have to change. They got her a tutor. Her room had to be tidy all the time. Nobody seemed interested in who she was anymore, only whether she did well. "I think so. Suddenly I was expected to be perfect."

"Your family may have been attempting to keep Angela alive through you. They simply transferred all of the dreams and goals they had for her onto you, as if by you accomplishing them, Angela would still be alive. Did they speak of her very much?"

"It was something we never mentioned." Margaret was quiet for some time.

"There's another problem in all this, Margaret." Dr. Lamont spoke slowly and with compassion. "Because you have buried your grief all this time, you haven't been able to express or even acknowledge your anger at having to live your sister's life instead of your own. To get angry would be to admit you have something to be angry about—your loss. In order to protect yourself from the pain of grief, you have been stifling your anger at how unfair everything is." She paused. "Any other losses more recently?"

Margaret looked up suddenly. "I just remembered. I had a miscarriage between the two girls. Nobody said anything much about it. I didn't either."

Dr. Lamont looked intent. "Miscarriage is a very difficult loss because no one recognizes it as such. It's a silent suffering among many women in our society."

Margaret sipped her tea and continued thinking. "Then there's my mother. She's only sixty-one, but she has been diagnosed as having cancer." Margaret looked at Dr. Lamont in sudden recognition. "There's the chance she might die."

◆ ◆ ◆

It was now evening. Margaret spread old family pictures and mementos out across her bedspread. There were pictures of her mother at a much younger age. The idea of her mother's life being over was nearly unthinkable. Even though she was an adult and herself a mother, Margaret could scarcely imagine the world without her mother. Margaret gathered all of the photos of her mother together.

There was an odd assortment of memorabilia from the second pregnancy, including a little boy's outfit she had purchased when she had first found out she was pregnant. They had even considered names. Todd. She had been so alone following the miscarriage.

There were some pictures of Angela, a few of herself, some with the both of them together. She realized there were quite a few more of Angela than of herself. Another interesting thing, she noted. Almost no pictures were taken after Angela's death.

There were also a number of newspaper clippings, report cards, awards and other documents. Most of these belonged to Angela. Those of her own were saved later, following Angela's death. It was almost as if she, Margaret, hadn't existed until Angela died.

Margaret thought about this. She remembered what Dr. Lamont had said about her having to live Angela's life. She hadn't believed it, or more accurately, hadn't really understood it at the time. Yet here, spread out before her, was evidence. Her parents had saved all of Angela's things, and only after Angela was no longer available had they started to save pictures and papers extolling Margaret's talents.

And Margaret hadn't really noticed. She reflected on the way in which pressure had increased yearly on her to get good grades, get on the honor roll, join the right clubs. She had been urged to play team sports, take part in school plays, join the local girls club. Even at fifteen years old, she was expected to choose the right college and declare a major. And never, never complain.

Margaret got a piece of paper and started a letter to her sister. She knew that Angela couldn't read it, but it seemed important to get some things off her chest. She wanted to let Angela know how she felt about her dying. At least let her know the little amount that she understood. And she wanted to let her know that at last she had some idea of the pressure under which Angela had lived. "Dear Angela," the letter began. "I've never written to you before, but here goes..."

◆ ◆ ◆

Margaret is discovering a whole new world because she is beginning to admit the losses she experienced and those she is facing. She finds that she has a reservoir of pain inside, of which she has been only dimly aware. She is learning that much of the way she had been treated as a child was related to her family's reaction to the loss of her sister. And finally, she can make the connection between her pain and losses and her pattern of compulsive eating.

Loss is as normal as growing up. Sometimes we fantasize a world in which there is no loss, no pain, but we know that such a world is inherently impossible. To grow means to encounter and attach to new things. Some of these we outgrow, some we must let go of as we pass from one stage in life to the next. We would have no room for art, music, cinema or the sorts of life commitments necessary for lasting satisfaction if we did not let go of nursing bottles, diapers, and the sandbox.

As we grow, we inevitably lose things. Important people may die or move away. We may leave a beloved place, or that place may change. We may outgrow comforting beliefs or values. Our parents may divorce or die and our children grow up and move away. Treasured objects may be stolen. Jobs may be lost, ideals shattered. Even our successes will bring about change. We cannot live and grow without experiencing loss.

If we are unable to let go of things that we have lost we become bound to the past. Clinging to what was in order to avoid the pain of loss, we stumble into the future backwards. As Margaret discovered, in order to resolve those early losses which blind us to the present, we must learn about the way our loss affected us.

A Time to Mourn

When we lose someone or something important to us, we move through a process of detachment so that we are free to reattach and love again. While we cannot replace a dear one, we must be able to reinvest ourselves in a new relationship. We must let go in order to move on, but this process of detachment is not easy.

Most therapists who have studied loss agree that

detachment occurs in stages. The first reaction to sudden loss is shock: we are taken by surprise, stunned by the news, and often quite disoriented. Our world is shaken. Things feel unreal. While we may have very strong initial emotional reactions, more often we are numb and unfeeling. We may become detached from things, or even unable to function. The shock may last from several hours to several days, and our ability to work and to parent may be compromised during this stage.

After the shock wears off, we pull ourselves together and go through the motions of coping and getting our lives back together. We alternate between functioning and falling apart. We may be greatly fatigued and have difficulty sleeping. We may feel anxiety, anger, or even guilt.

In order to manage the intensity of our feelings, we may deny the severity or even reality of the loss itself. We may minimize the importance of the loss, or distort it in our thinking. Our mind, body, feelings, and behavior all show upset as we struggle to comprehend and accept the loss. Like Margaret, we may progress no further in our grieving than this. We live in such a way as to avoid feeling more than this, and can put the grieving on hold indefinitely.

Once we work through denial, the reality of the loss becomes real, and we reach the next stage. Loss is hurt, and the natural response to hurt is anger. We may direct our anger at the circumstance of loss or even at the lost person. Alternatively, we may displace anger upon others or even upon ourselves. The depth of the anger and the difficulty of its expression depends upon the temperament of the griever and the extent and nature of the loss. In any case, the emergence of anger is a clear indication that we are feeling the loss, and is most likely temporary.

Margaret did not remember her first reactions of

shock, nor her later feelings of sadness, until she worked with Dr. Lamont. She had shut down on her feelings of loss because it was too painful, and because her family demanded it. With her counselor's help, Margaret learned that she had to let go of her loss or remain chained to the past, uncertain of the future, and dysfunctioning in the present.

To progress in our grieving means suffering. The next stage of mourning is depression, in which we experience loneliness, helplessness, and exhaustion as well as fears about facing an uncertain world. We begin to question whether or not our reasons to go on are greater than the pain we must endure. Now that Margaret has opened herself to this suffering, she can complete her grieving. She can turn around her eating problem because she no longer needs the emotional cushion it once provided her. She is free to be open to her life.

In order to complete the process of fully accepting loss, we must put the relationship into proper perspective. The meaning of the relationship must be understood and honored, and then it must be given over to the past. Emotionally we must clean house. We must express whatever emotions have resulted from the loss, including owning up to both the good and the bad. We must complete unfinished business, including saying things unsaid, doing things undone, and letting go of the rest. This often results in deep sorrow and even depression.

Your behavior may be hard to change if you have suffered loss and your grieving is unfinished. You may be either trying to ease your pain or to avoid making commitments in your life by engaging in destructive behavior.

If this is so, your ability to grow will depend upon facing up to your prior loss. To do this takes courage and perseverance. You will need to spend time developing awareness of the loss and remembering the events surrounding it. Feelings—past and current—must be expressed. Telling the story of the loss and its meaning is as important in dealing with loss as it is with prior trauma.

Contrary to popular belief, grieving your past losses does not need to be painful or lengthy. You are used to the pain already; it has fashioned your life and your addiction. Understanding helps a great deal, as does revisiting important places. Relaxation and imagery can be very useful in making the memories more bearable. Sharing the pain with others is helpful as well.

Finally, there is another, different way in which loss affects us. If we are trying to let go of destructive behavior, we must appreciate that that, too, is a loss. Our "problem" was once a solution. It gave us comfort, relief, excitement. If it hadn't, we wouldn't have allowed it to become a part of our lives. Now we are trying to cut it out of our life. If Margaret wants to give up the abuse of food, she must face up to the loss involved. Otherwise, she will not understand why she sabotages her own recovery. As strange as it sounds, grieving the loss of our compulsion or addiction is part of the solution.

The questions in the following sections are meant to be done in order. To benefit the most from working on them, it would be very helpful if you kept a journal or notebook. Find one that feels right, and make a paragraph or page entry every day. This will not only pull things together, but it will be an interesting document for you later. Write about your reactions to the exercises, memories that come up, conversations you have, feelings you experience, and even dreams you have during this time.

Another good idea is to pick someone who would be a good listener. Choose someone you can talk to every now and then about your work in this chapter. If you worked through the last chapter on trauma, you probably already have people picked out.

The questions and discussions in the next section are written as if the loss you experienced was a person, such as a parent, sibling, or friend. If your loss was of a place, time, object, or relationship, reword the questions appropriately.

Signs of Unresolved Loss

Begin by identifying whether you experience signs that there are losses which still bother you. If you experience any of the following symptoms, you may suffer from unresolved loss:

unhappiness
irritability
depression
difficulty with relationships
problems at work
compulsions or dependencies
acting out
attitude and mood problems
underperformance
lack of personal growth
avoidance of painful issues
avoidance of good-byes
avoidance of throwing things away
inability to make life changes
inability to take reasonable risks
inability to help others change and develop
periods of unexplained sadness or crying
avoidance or fear of new "loves"

You may also experience the following symptoms related to an experience of someone's death:

flashbacks
avoidance of certain locations, situations, themes
specific fears, anxieties, preoccupations
nightmares
attempts to relive and master the incident

If you have experienced some of these latter signs, the death or the initial experience of the loss may have been traumatic for you. You may benefit from going back and working through the previous chapter, "Letting Go of Past Hurt." If the death was traumatic for you, resolving the loss is likely to be delayed until the reactions to the trauma have subsided.

Identifying Losses

While some people have never experienced significant losses in their lives, most of us have suffered major losses by the time we have reached twenty-five. Some have experienced many such losses. Here is a chance to identify the various losses in your life. Some possible losses you may wish to consider are:

death of a parent
remarriage/stepsiblings
death of a relative
loss of physical capabilities
death of a friend or teacher
death of a spouse
serious illness/hospitalization

relocation
divorce/separation
friend/family relocation
boarding school
change of school
foster home
new sibling who parents favor
theft/home destruction
community change
loss of love relationship

While you might not consider some of the above losses major, realize that not only are losses subjective, varying in intensity from person to person, but they are also cumulative. A series of small losses can have as great an effect as one large loss.

Focus upon the loss which you remember to be the worst. Think for a moment about this loss, considering what that person had meant to you prior to his or her death.

- ♦ Write three significant incidents you remember that involve that person.
- ♦ How much did he or she mean to you?
- ♦ Do you have any other special memories of that person, particularly memories involving the rest of your family?

After you complete the chapter, you will probably wish to go back and repeat the exercises for each of the other losses you have listed above as being serious for you.

Living through the Dying

What do you remember about the moment of loss? Depending upon the type of loss, this may have been a death, the end of a relationship, a move, or the moment you heard of your loss. What events do you remember happening, and what do you remember doing?

Can you remember how you felt when your loved one died, or after you heard about the death? Use the list of feelings on page 99 as a reminder. In your notebook, write down the feelings you experienced, putting short phrases where possible.

Was there a funeral or memorial service? Did you attend? Do you remember anything about it? Write down any particular memories (sights, sounds, impressions, reflections) you might have of the moment. Can you recall how you felt at the time?

A eulogy is a reflection upon a person's life. It includes basic biographical information such as birth date, hometown, family and career statistics, and major events in his or her life. It also tries to comment upon the significance and meaning of the life. Find the eulogy from the funeral if available. Add to it from your own memories. If one is not available, write one yourself.

Another project you might try is to make a scrapbook about the person lost. This could serve as a living memory and will provide relatives and descendants with an idea of just what he or she was like. You could include the eulogy you have written, letters, clippings, photographs, testimonies from others, or any other mementos.

What the Loss Has Meant

Any significant loss has implications for those who suffered the loss. The information gathered here will give clues to what the loss has meant in your life during the years since the death.

On a page in your journal, draw a time line like the one in the diagram. Mark the major events that have occurred in your life since the person's death:

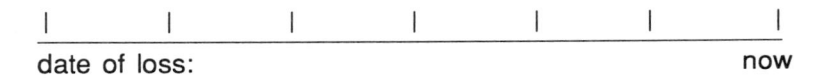

date of loss: now

If the South had won the Civil War, if the Japanese had not bombed Pearl Harbor, if John F. Kennedy had not won the presidency, things might have been very different for the United States. The same is true for you. Things might have been very different had your loss not occurred. Sit back for a moment and speculate.

- Might things have been easier or harder? Might you have developed differently? Might you have made different choices in your life?

- If this person was really important to you, then you had part of your life tied up in him or her. You may have identified with him or her, or perhaps you were in some way dependent on her or him. If nothing else, the death may have meant some change in your way of life. Looking at it from this perspective, what part of your life was lost when he or she died?

- How about the rest of your family? Have they changed their feelings, interactions, or expectations regarding one another as a result of the loss? How has the loss affected them as individuals and how has it affected your life together?

- Sometimes a loss is very painful. So painful, in fact, that we can't talk about it even with those who are close to us. And when we can't do that, it can drive a wedge between us. Who haven't you talked about the loss with (either in your family or outside of it)? Is this something you need to do?

Grieving

You may have great sadness and pain locked inside of you. Grieving is the process of expressing the feelings that loss has created. Mourning is sometimes complicated by mixed feelings, unfinished relationships, feelings of anger, betrayal, disappointment, or confusion. These complications serve to confuse and diffuse the pure expression of grief.

If you get stuck on this section and find it too hard to do, or if you find yourself overwhelmed by the feelings the exercises generate, do yourself a favor and get some assistance. Find a counselor whose job is to help people express, heal, and learn from their reactions. Life is too short to waste because of embarrassment, false pride, or fear!

Here are some things you can do to help let the feelings out:

- Visit important places you and the person whom you lost shared together. Make entries for each visit, like the form on page 124. Fill out the questions while you are there.

....

Visitation

Date: _____ Place: _____

I remember coming here with (who:) _____

(when:) _____

I remember the following things happening: _____

_____

_____

Being here now, I am feeling: _____

_____

_____

I need: _____

_____

_____

....

- Do something you liked to do together. Fill out the same visitation form.

- Visit the grave if possible. Imagine that he or she can talk to you. Begin by sharing all of the things you have written so far. Let your conversation ramble, and catch him or her up on your life. Leave feelings of embarrassment and self-consciousness at home, because this is much more important to you than anything others might think.

- Write a letter from the person who died to the rest of the world. In it, imagine that you are that person, writing to explain why you lived the life you did. It could be titled, "In my defense."

- Spend some time interviewing people who knew the person. Find out how they saw him or her, interesting anecdotes they can recall, and what he or she meant to them.

- Write the deceased a letter. Tell him or her what he or she meant to you. Express how you felt about the death and how you feel now. Bring up any unfinished business, and say any things that were left unsaid. Say good-bye.

- Hold a ritual reburial. Put copies of the letter or other mementos in a box and bury it, burn it, or take it somewhere and leave it. Dress appropriately for the occasion, and have a speech and prayers prepared. Consider inviting others, particularly family members along. Spend time giving vent to feelings.

- Find a way to forgive the deceased for any offenses against you, and apologize for any offenses you may have committed against him or her.

- Set aside time alone in which to cry, express anger, or whatever else comes up. Light candles, play appropriate music. Let your feelings loose.

- Share your experiences doing these exercises and your grief with a listener and others close to you.

This process will take time. Start it now and continue it as you work through the book, knowing that the grieving process may take months or even years to complete. Realize that grieving is an essentially healthy process. Despite its pain, grieving allows you to detach from your past and focus your energy on the remaining things and people in your life. Opening to the future requires putting the past to rest.

Rituals, Memorials, and Rebuilding

Ever since this loss, you have been building your future. If the unresolved loss kept you from growing, the future you have been creating has been artificially limited in some ways. Once you find release from the bonds of the past, you are free to fashion a richer future.

One reason we resist letting go of important people is that they provide support and direction for us. If they were important, it was because they met some of our needs. If we let them go, those needs must still be met, and we must find new ways to meet them.

For thousands of years people have used purification rituals to cleanse "ghosts and evil spirits" out of their lives and minds. A ritual cleansing can be a creative act with deep psychological benefits, and you can design one for yourself. Be especially attuned to your feeling during the ritual, and don't be afraid to weep, say things that have been left unsaid, or express whatever feelings may come up.

Another good way of rebuilding the future is to create a memorial project, which seals off the past while bringing the best of that past into the future. What is a life about? What is the point of having lived if nothing is changed as a result of that life? Realistically, no monument or edifice is likely to last very long. Yet it is unsatisfying to watch those whom we have loved and cared for slide quickly into obscurity. One of the most terrifying aspects of our own mortality is the prospect that our lives do not matter and that the world was no different as the result of our having lived. Often our unresolved grieving is a misguided attempt to forestall such oblivion. It is both fitting and fulfilling to create a lasting work in the world in honor of the deceased. These memorials may include donations to causes, endowments, commitments of time to projects, completion of tasks left undone, or any other ways in which the interests and energy of the deceased are honored and commemorated.

Whatever way you chose to rebuild your life without the person you lost, you must put that person's contribution to your life in perspective. That person was important to you because he or she gave you something special. What personal traits, values, and resources did you gain from the person who was lost which you can use in meeting the future you wish to fashion?

Sometimes first attempts at resolving past losses prove to be only partially successful. One indication is persistent symptoms of grief, which you identified earlier in these exercises. There may be other losses you still need to deal with, or you may need to do more work. Try repeating the exercises with greater openness to the feelings. If you are still unable to move forward you should consider seeing a counselor or attending a grief group in your community. Also, family pressures may be working against your efforts. If that is so, the next chapter, "Taking Care of Family Business," may be helpful.

7

Taking Care of Family Business

Home is where the heart is, our source of nurture, our sanctuary from life. Or at least it can be. For many the reality may be very different. For many the family is not only the original source of their dysfunction, but also the major obstacle standing between them and getting well. This chapter can help you deal with:

- **Childhood family of origin experiences** that shape your expectations, reactions, and even perceptions right now. These color how you approach your career, your relationships, and even yourself.

- **Current family of origin relationships** that affect you now. Outmoded family patterns are hard to break. Roles, scripts, and ongoing dramas are continually reinforced, strengthening resistance to change.

- **Spousal or significant other relationships.** When you are tired, stressed out, or overwhelmed, you may react to your spouse or significant other as if he or she was your parent. In other words, you may tend to reenact your own early parent/child interactions without realizing it.

- **Children.** Your relationship with your children is shaped and influenced by your experiences as a child, and your perceptions of what it means to be a good parent.

◆ ◆ ◆

Brad is a chronic gambler. Several months have passed since he completed a recovery program and he continues follow-up sessions with a counselor.

Brad knocked on Frank's door before opening it. "Come in," Frank's voice called, and Brad entered. Brad valued his sessions with Frank, and was rarely late. He had raced to get to this one on time, and was still trying to catch his breath.

"Sit down, Brad. It's good to see you." Frank put down the case report he was reviewing. "You look winded. How are you doing?"

"I don't know, a little nervous, out of balance. It's probably the holidays coming up."

"To be expected. Lots of extra demands, extra stress. Lot's of demands we make on ourselves..."

"I'm afraid of relapse. I don't know if I can stay clean and sober. My condo seems especially empty this time of year, and there are so many parties."

"Good! You should be afraid. It's not going to be easy." Frank smiled one of his clear "I-understand-and-it's-still-your-responsibility" smiles.

Brad looked quizzically at Frank. "In general, or for me in particular?"

"For you in particular. Two problems. One is your lack

of close friends and support. It worries me that I'm the closest thing you've got to a friend. The other is your family." He shifted and continued, "You've come a long, long way in this program. Through your own efforts and faith, you've been able to turn things around."

Brad smiled. It felt good to hear it. He had come to trust Frank's compliments and not look for some kind of ulterior motive.

"Remember when we talked about parents?" Frank asked. "We said that the single most important thing they could provide was consistency."

"Yeah, I do," acknowledged Brad, "and my parents were not consistent. They painted a great face—looking good to others—but when my father drank, and when they would fight, I got ignored. Sometimes I had to take care of myself for days.

"Brad, your gambling was, is, your attempt to gain control over how you felt. By controlling the risks of the external reality through gambling, you attempted to control your inner reality—your feelings, and experience. To a certain extent it worked. Now, staying clean depends upon finding better ways to control your reality."

Frank continued. "Your family hasn't changed. You are going to have to learn how to handle your reactions to their pressure on you in order to stay clean. It's going to be tough, because you not only have to fight your urge to gamble, but also your family."

"I know," admitted Brad. "It's been that way for a long time. And that worries me, Frank. It's almost Thanksgiving and I'm going back home for the holiday. I'm not sure what to expect from them. I've got a feeling that I'm not going to be able to tell them much about what I've learned here."

They were quiet for a time, each into his own thoughts. Their conversations were like those between old friends.

Frank spoke first. "Remember that time we talked about family resistance to change?" Brad nodded.

"We said that some families actually work at keeping their members dysfunctioning." Frank shifted in his chair, leaning toward Brad. "This is going to be like a game. A very serious game. Your recovery will depend upon whether you can figure out why they need you to have a problem, and how they work to keep you gambling."

◆ ◆ ◆

"Hi. My name is Luke, and I am an alcoholic and addict. This is the regular meeting of Overcomers Anonymous."

"Hi, Luke..." came the reply from the fifteen or so members sitting around in a circle.

Luke continued. "For those of you who are new, Overcomers Anonymous is a nonprofit organization whose purpose..." Brad was surprised at how similar this meeting was to those at Memorial. He was nervous about attending, but at the same time relieved there was a meeting to go to. He wasn't sure what else he would have done.

"Tonight we're going to talk about 'Enabling.'" said Luke. "I know that I personally have struggled with an enabler all my married life, and that I have struggled with being an enabler myself. Has anyone else ever lived with someone who helped them do what they shouldn't do?"

As several people spoke about enablers in their lives, Brad thought about his. His parents made it so easy for him. They gave him the motivation: gambling had been a way to strike back at them. They couldn't stop him, and had looked the other way, covered up for him, excused his behavior, and constantly bailed him out of debts to protect their own image. He had appreciated the enabling and certainly used it. Now it was dawning on him just how damaging the enabling had been.

"Has anyone else had a difficult time because of enablers?" Luke asked the group. No one spoke. The silence was uncomfortable, but Brad fought against the impulse to break it. What could he possibly offer? He didn't really even know what he would say.

"I have," Brad heard himself say. "My parents always told me not to screw around, but never drew the line unless it inconvenienced them. Tonight it became clear to me how difficult it was to grow up in that family." Brad's voice broke, but he controlled it and kept on. "I'm scared that I won't be able to handle it. I'm afraid I'll blow recovery. I'm also afraid that I'll never want a family of my own."

"Brad," Luke spoke softly, "it makes us sad to find out that our parents weren't what we needed them to be, or that they actually helped us keep our compulsion then and make it easy for us to go back to it now. But sometimes that's just the way it is. I ask myself the question, 'Does this person need me to dysfunction?' Or sometimes I ask, 'What does my dysfunction buy them?' When others are invested in my having a problem, I have to find a way to protect myself. What can you do to protect yourself from your family?"

♦ ♦ ♦

It was late in the evening when Brad got home. The phone was ringing and he picked it up. It was his father, who sounded as if he had been drinking.

"Where have you been? I've been calling for an hour. It's midnight here."

"At a meeting." To his surprise, Brad's father seemed to accept this. Brad asked, "How's Mom?"

"She's gone to bed. She's tired." He didn't say anything for a moment. Then he spoke again. "We had a fight." This admission surprised Brad again.

Brad remained quiet. "I don't know," his father continued.

"It doesn't even matter what it was about. We seem to fight just to fight." He waited for Brad to say something. With Brad's assistance not forthcoming, he went on. "I've been thinking. Maybe we should see a counselor. What do you think?"

Brad sensed that his father was about to try and get him involved. He answered with compassion and detachment. "I hope you can work it out, Dad. Good night."

◆ ◆ ◆

During the course of his recovery, Brad found that his family of origin could not help him. Further, he found that his early experiences had much to do with his tendency to avoid significant relationships. While he knows that he is still responsible for his own life, these awarenesses help him understand his past and plan for his future.

Not everyone who has a problem comes from a problem family. But a great many do! Understanding your family is important for three reasons:

- Your early family experiences may have a lot to do with why you *started* your problem behavior.

- Your family of origin may have a lot to do with why you *keep* your problem behavior.

- Both your family of origin and your current family may actually work against you in *getting rid* of your problem.

Families are quite complicated. To get a better understanding of how to deal with them, it helps to have some basic concepts. First, we need to understand that families are systems. This means that they consist of interconnected parts, and that the functioning of each part will affect each other part.

When you think about it, the idea that your family would work at keeping you dysfunctioning makes no sense, particularly if your dysfunction hurts them. But look at it this way: the family, just like any organization, must be able to count on routine.

This routine involves shared expectations. Like a racing pit crew, each family member needs to be able to count on a certain predictability. Our roles within the family define what we can expect from others and what others can expect from us. Each role, once worked out, has a place in maintaining the complex order of family life. Consequently, each family member is encouraged—even pressured—to fulfill his or her role. Even in families where an individual is cast in a "sick" role (like "the drinker," or "the gambler") the other family members have spent a great deal of time and energy working out their own roles to accommodate that person. This allows them to go on with their lives without having to stop and remodel everything.

While healthy families encourage gradual growth and change within members, this may not be so with struggling families. Such change creates demands for adjustment. In unhealthy families, the drive for stability strangles individual change. Even change for the better is resisted. Family traditions can become stagnant, communication can be restricted, and stony silence and rigidity may replace support. While the family members would never admit to themselves that they did not support recovery, their day-to-day behavior can create tremendous road-blocks to change. Further, your problem behavior may be important to family members who may use it to avoid their own change. They may welcome a diversion, because they get to treat your problem as if it were *the* family problem.

Here are some general strategies for dealing with family members who seem to be working against your recovery:

- Awareness is the best defense. Whenever you are running into family difficulties that are making recovery hard, ask yourself, "In what way could this be protecting my family members from having to make their own changes?"

- Consider the possibility that their resistance might be the result of misunderstanding. Ask yourself, "Have I made my intentions clear?" and, "Do they know why I am doing what I am doing?"

- Examine the way you are approaching them. Are you being too forceful, too unbending? Have you given them a chance to be heard? Have you really let them know that you have heard them? Think about whether you are being unnecessarily inflammatory. Ask, "Am I using terms or language that distracts them from the real issues?"

- Consider the effects of your actions upon each of the other family members.

- Anticipate their fears. Reassure them about what you are *not* going to do.

- Don't try to challenge them about their own defects of character. Lead by example.

If you really want to change some things about yourself, you have to start by figuring out your family's role in your problem. What was the general climate of your early family life? Some families are generally supportive, challenging, loving, or strong. Others are not. Troubled families can raise children who reflect that trouble. While it is true some children are simply more resilient than others, it nevertheless helps to get a picture of your family's climate in order to understand the family origins of your problem behavior.

Early Family Experiences

Parents build families and shape children. If they do a reasonable job, the children generally thrive and grow strong. In fact, it is amazing just how many parenting mistakes children can take without developing lasting problems. There are limits, however, and children can suffer harm through consistently poor parenting.

Some types of parenting are particularly hard on kids. If you grew up with parents who were so involved with their own problems that they didn't have the time or energy to give you what you needed, you may still be needy. If they were unable to provide consistency or leadership, you may be still seeking it. If you grew up unloved, you may spend your days in a fruitless search for love.

All of us need to believe in our parents, particularly if we have reason to doubt them. So we tend to be over-forgiving and deny their faults. This means that we blame ourselves for our shortcomings. But look at it this way. It is one thing to accept responsibility for what you need to change; that is good. It is quite another, however, to deny how you got that way. That keeps you from changing. You need to understand the origins of your dysfunction in order to begin addressing it.

Some specific personal profiles have been associated with particular parent styles. Think about your experience as you review the list on the next page.

Parenting styles contribute to the general climate of the home. The four general family climates that lead to

Do any of these profiles fit you?	If so, your parents may have been:
anxious (insecure, negative, hostile, lacking self-esteem, jealous)	rejecting
submissive (dependent upon others, lacking in self-esteem, slow, lacking self-reliance)	overprotecting, dominating
impulsive (selfish, demanding, rebellious, lacking responsibility, unable to tolerate frustration)	overpermissive, overindulgent
rigid (guilt-ridden, lacking spontaneity, conflicted, overly conscientious, self-condemning, needing to please, procrastinating)	perfectionistic, demanding
lost (confused, lacking self-identity or initiative, having a poor self-image, looking for stable values)	inconsistent, inadequate
angry (having problems with friends, hating parents, aggressive, fighting authority, self-destructive)	over-punishing

later problems for the children are weak, hostile, disturbed, or broken. See if your own family fits one of the four problem profiles:

- **Weak**

    The weak family is unable to provide strong leadership, guidance, resources and support to its children. This may be due to the parents' lack of ability or resources, or both. Such a family has difficulty coping with ordinary problems of living, lacks resources, and requires outside assistance. Family members often have certain inadequacies (mental, maturational, educational) resulting in incompetence. They have trouble adjusting to changes, or are unable to provide their children with security and guidance. Weak families are often unable to assist in the development of basic competencies that are vital to self-esteem.

- **Hostile**

    The hostile family lives by and for conflict. As a result, children are subjected to a climate of fear where they are denied the opportunity to develop their talents in a supportive, nurturing environment. There is a great deal of fighting, nagging, belittling, or annoying behavior in the family, and family members experience much frustration and dissatisfaction. Communication is often poor, and there is often a lack of consistency in the enforcement of rules. Children are unable to learn to communicate, trust, or establish solid relationships.

- **Crazy/Addicted**

    The crazy or addicted family is erratic, inconsistent, and in turmoil. One or both parents may be emotionally disturbed, or dependent upon some sort of substance or compulsive behavior, but sometimes it is just the interaction itself that is crazy. Children growing up in such a home are deprived of stability and predictability and have little chance of security. There is usually a great deal of emotional turmoil, which starts easily and never resolves anything. Children are often pulled into the emotional conflicts between parents, and the disharmony results in a constant threat to family security.

- **Broken**

    The broken family often lacks the sense of secure continuity that a two-parent family can provide. Whether the break-up occurred because of death or by choice, children can be left without the support they are used to. The children often feel conflicting loyalties and pressure to prefer one parent over the other, and may live in fear of rejection and abandonment. One parent may be so caught up in his or her own grief that he or she is emotionally unavailable. As a result, the children may experience deprivation of stability or deprivation of love.

In families such as these, often at least one of the parents is alcoholic, violent, depressed, or has some other disability that renders her or him unable to parent. A word often used to describe this person is "dysfunctional," which means she or he cannot function the way she or he should.

A family with a dysfunctional parent might still be able to handle the situation. Often, however, the other parent is not able to cope well, either. Sometimes he or she falls apart. Sometimes he or she is unable to force the dysfunctional parent to get help. Whatever the reason, a parent who allows the other parent to continue dysfunctioning is called an "enabler." The enabler lets the dysfunction go on and adds to the stress on the children.

Children and Coping

A child growing up in a family that fits one of the above profiles has to do considerable adjusting and adapting. From the child's point of view, family rules in a dysfunctional family are sometimes nonexistent, sometimes over-enforced. Sometimes the parents are present and supportive, sometimes not. Sometimes home is a safe place to be, and sometimes it is dangerous.

Your personal style of coping

When your family was stressful to you—when they were hostile, weak, crazy, or broken—how did you protect yourself? If your family fit one of these styles, you probably worked out a system of coping with the stress. How healthy was your coping style?

Children need security, structure, stability, and consistency to flourish. When those attributes are not available, they take defensive action and find ways to make the best of it for themselves.

Four basic styles of coping are common among children of hostile, weak, crazy or broken families. This account of these styles is adapted from the work of therapist Sharon Wegsheider-Cruse.

Superachiever

When the family cannot consistently meet the needs of the children, one child often takes over the parental tasks. This is often the oldest child, or the second child if a girl. The superachiever sometimes cooks, does laundry, supervises homework, and puts the other children to bed. Often the superachiever holds a job and uses the money to provide food. The superachiever grows up too quickly.

This role carries two major problems. First, as a mini-parent, the superachiever is deprived of a normal childhood. Second, because the parents have all of those obligations met for them, they stay dysfunctional.

In deciding whether you became the family's superachiever, ask yourself: Did I spend more time taking care of others than myself? When my parents were unable, did I cook, wash, and do the household tasks they should have done? Did I feel responsible for a parent's problems? Did others in my family want me to take care of their problems? Did I go on to be a high achiever? Do I tend to take things too seriously? Do I feel that I must constantly earn others' love?

Problem child

When children's needs go continually unmet and they are deprived of affection and security, they get angry. Sometimes they act out that anger by getting in trouble. They may get rebellious and defy authority, or they become aggressive or destructive. Others may turn their anger inward, becoming depressed or even self-destructive. Delinquency, problems at school, substance abuse, and emotional difficulties all serve to send angry messages and gain attention.

Ask yourself: Was I the one in the family labeled the "problem child"? Did I spend lots of time at the doctor's, counselor's, or principal's office? Did I have problems with teachers and school work? Did I have run-ins with the police? Did I get into early substance abuse? Do I continue to get into trouble? Did I or do I have problems with relationships with others? Do I have emotional problems?

Low-profile child

When the family is unstable and things become uncomfortable, crazy, or even violent, one good way of dealing is to keep out of harm's way. The low-profile child has made this approach a whole lifestyle. This person doesn't say much, blends into the woodwork, and hides when conflicts arise.

Ask yourself: Did I or do I avoid conflicts when possible? Did I spend a lot of time by myself? Did I or do I avoid leadership positions? Do I hold back? Do I avoid confronting others, even when it's important? Am I more afraid of being left than being hurt? Do I feel guilty or vulnerable if I stand up for myself? Do I let myself get hurt in relationships? Do I have trouble standing up for my children?

Clown or baby

Another role is the family baby or clown. This is often a youngest sibling or one who is treated as "special." This child is not held to the same expectations as the others and is cushioned from the problems. The baby survives by being cute, or funny, often playing the part of the clown.

Ask yourself: Was I the "special one?" Was I able to get away with things my other siblings were unable to get away with? Was I able to turn away hostility or conflict by being funny? Did I gain support by being "cute" or charming? In school, was I the class clown? Do I still try to charm people and get my way by winning them over? Is it important, or safest, for me to be the center of attention? Do I continue to use interpersonal charm and influence to achieve my ends at home or at work?

You may find that sometimes you alternate between one coping style and another, or go from one to another as you grow older. Often your addiction—that you now want to change—started as part of your coping style.

One mark of a dysfunctional family is the way the children assume these roles as part of their identity. If your own children are taking these roles, this may be an indication that they are under stress due to your problem behavior. Does your parenting or family style fit one of those described earlier? If so, your child might benefit from early intervention by a family therapist.

A major difficulty of taking on a particular role is that the family expects it of you and pressures you not to change. When you try to turn around behavior patterns that you no longer accept in yourself, your family members often are the ones to sabotage your efforts.

Managing Your Parents and Siblings

Whether your changes are for the better or for worse, they will affect the lives of other family members, and your spouse, parents, or children will probably try to cushion the blow. This means that the difficult changes in your life will be made all the harder. When changing results in family resistance, it feels a little like swimming upstream. The current is against you, and sometimes it slows you down or forces you back. Like salmon leaping over small waterfalls, you may have to try some tricks to get around the resistance.

Here are some suggestions for dealing with family members who are holding you back:

- **Look beyond the behavior to see the need.** When people hold you back, it is usually because they have a personal investment in things staying the same. They may need security, attention, or something else, and your change threatens their need. Think about the real need that motivates them.

- **Reassure the real need.** Looking at the real need, what could you say or do to help satisfy that need without compromising your need to change?

- **Hang tough.** Change takes time, and overcoming resistance takes a lot of time. In order for you to get what you want, you cannot give up until you get past the attempts to hold you back. What can you do to help yourself hang in there?

- **Get some support outside the system.** You need someone to acknowledge your efforts, celebrate your successes, and sustain you through the struggle. When your family can't give you that support, you need to get it somewhere else. Consider reaching out to your group, friends, or a professional.

Changing Your Personal Style

What is the best way of coping with tough family situations? It depends. A good strategy in one situation might be terrible in another. Being assertive in a hostile situation may set you up for an assault. Keeping a low profile when you are being ignored or abandoned may keep you from getting what you need. Here are four powerful coping styles, but keep in mind that, they are only powerful in the right place!

Assertive

Being assertive means standing up for your rights. It means not being passive and not letting yourself be pushed around. But it also means not being aggressive. The difference between aggression and assertion has to do with personal rights. Aggression is when you stand up for your rights and ignore the rights of others. Assertion is when you stand up for your rights without depriving others of theirs. To be assertive means to speak out in defense of yourself.

Here are five ways to be assertive:

1. Avoid aggressive or passive behavior.

2. In any situation, ask yourself, "What do I want here?" or "What would be best for me?" Make your needs known.

3. Use the "broken record" technique: if someone is giving you all sorts of reasons why you shouldn't get what you need, keep repeating, "That may be the case, but I want _____." Don't be distracted, don't get out of control.

4. Make long-range plans for getting what you want. Write down all that needs to be done, first things first.

5. When you need others to do things for you, or to treat you differently, make formal requests for change: sit down with them; tell them exactly what they are doing now that affects you badly; tell them exactly how it affects you when they do it; describe exactly what you would like them to do differently; request that they do it. (For example: "Would you please do such-and-such?")

Remember that being assertive is a habit. It will feel strange at first. If you have been passive in the past, being assertive will feel as if you are being aggressive. Get someone who knows your family situation to serve as an objective bystander and coach.

Self-contained

Being self-contained has to do with no longer being an enabler. If you take responsibility for others and allow them to act in ways that are bad for them or for you, you are helping them to stay stuck. Being self-contained means taking responsibility for your actions and letting others be responsible for their own. When the other family members rely on you to take care of them, they are not doing either you or themselves a favor. To be self-contained is to look out for yourself and not take care of others when they can take care of themselves.

Here are five ways to be self-contained:

1. Take care of your own needs first.

2. Be clear about responsibility; know the limits of your responsibility.

3. Avoid enabling behaviors; ask yourself, "Will my

doing this help this person to stay _____ (helpless/drunk/abusive/out of control)?"

4. Carry out your own obligations.

5. Find people outside your family who will help you get what you need and can coach you in dealing with family members.

Low profile

Some situations are dangerous, physically or emotionally. When dealing with crazy, violent, or drunk people, it sometimes makes more sense to stay out of their way. Why get hurt if it will not change anything? To keep a low profile means to avoid standing out and attracting pointless abuse. This is a particularly powerful strategy in those situations where the problems occur in cycles. Be assertive when the violence or conflict is not a problem, but keep a low profile when it becomes mindless and intense.

Here are five ways to maintain a low profile:

1. Become aware of cycles of hostility or craziness; when such conflicts occur, leave.

2. Avoid high traffic areas and areas of conflict.

3. Only enter into discussions that are positive or have a strong likelihood of being productive.

4. Find out how to get help from the outside, if needed.

5. Look for indirect ways to get your needs met.

Detached

If your needs are not being met at home, you need to take better care of yourself. This means becoming less dependent on home for your emotional (and sometimes physical) support. Distance yourself, become more detached. This is a more extreme version of being self-contained and requires reaching outside the family for assistance.

Here are five ways to become more detached:

1. Develop goals and attachments apart from the family.
2. Create a strong support system outside the family.
3. Learn to get your rewards from people outside the family.
4. Avoid being pulled into family conflicts or flaps.
5. Find "chosen family" and spend time with them.

Again, these four different approaches are powerful, but only in the right settings. And they are suggestions only; each individual and situation is unique and there is no formula for success. Each of us must work out his or her own best way.

The chart on page 149 offers a place for you to begin. Your plan could apply to either your current family or your family of origin. First, find your *present* coping style on the left side. The adaptive goal shown next to it is where you want to get to. The next four columns show the strategy you should use to get there. Find your family climate at the top. Match the style with the climate, and you have your general direction. For example, if you are the problem child in a hostile family you probably should

Charting Your Way

Personal Coping Style	Your Adaptive Goal	If your family climate is...			
		weak	hostile	crazy/ addicted	broken
		...your strategy is to try and be			
super-achiever	learning to let go	self-contained	low profile	detached	assertive
problem child	learning to be OK	self-contained	low profile	low profile	assertive
low-profile	learning to speak out	assertive	self-contained	detached	assertive
baby/ clown	learning to get serious	assertive	self-contained	self-contained	assertive

work at developing a low-profile style. This would help you handle the situation the best possible way.

Now look at the power style the chart recommends for you. Reread the description of the style and the ways to start. Think about how those strategies might work for you in your situation. Consider specific ways you could do each of those things. What else could you do to further your power style?

Consider this list a plan of attack. Use it. Copy it on a card and carry it around in your pocket until you need it, then pull it out to remind yourself of what to do.

Treat this like any other plan, and watch to see which parts work the best. You may soon find yourself handling those difficult family interactions better than you had ever dreamed possible!

Recovery is difficult. Family relationships stretch and ultimately transform. Learn, experiment, and become strong at dealing with your family. Do not expect overnight miracles. Be patient, keep trying new strategies, and stay with your struggle toward independence from the habits and dependencies of the past. Consider also that professional assistance from a family therapist, particularly one who is versed in recovery needs, could be very useful in assisting you to revitalize your primary relationship.

Living in the Present: Recapitulation and Adaptive Style

As Hal Stone and Sidra Winkler point out in *Embracing Each Other*, we often fall in love only to find ourselves growing apart. The early fire of our love relationship which brings such liberation, release, and promise seems over time to extinguish itself under the weight of our lives. What we initially perceived as being challenge and excitement seems to wither into burden and conflict. Our optimism and joy turn to sadness and frustration as we try time and time again to resurrect the love—only to find ourselves falling back into destructive patterns.

Many of these patterns are distressingly familiar. On closer examination they turn out to be old battles fought previously with our parents when we were much younger. It is as if the sensitivities and vulnerabilities of our youth have transported themselves into our present relationship, creating a virtual minefield at home.

Stone and Winkler show how recognizing recurring interpersonal struggles as an interlocking pattern of personal conflict can provide the awareness necessary to transform those struggles into personal growth. The adaptive strategies outlined in this chapter can help in changing our counterproductive behaviors. As a responsible parent, you should also observe your children's adaptive styles. If you see how a different style may empower them, encourage and coach their efforts to learn that new approach to dealing with family circumstances.

Parenting through Times of Transition

One of the hardest aspects of parenting is that parents are never off duty. For better or worse, in sickness and in health, and during times of personal tumult and change, parents must still parent. This is particularly difficult for those parents who are deeply into the process of reevaluating their own childhood experiences, acknowledging and coming to grips with their own childhood needs, and questioning the manner in which they have created and contributed to current family problems.

During these times of self-examination and vulnerability, parents must continue to make parental decisions, set and enforce family rules, and provide the warmth, security, and support their children need. These are times of self-doubt, intense feelings, and changing standards. And, of course this is precisely when our children's needs are greatest.

In general, consistency in rules, consequences, and your reactions is a virtue. The following suggestions may help you navigate through stormy waters:

- ♦ Sort out the issues you are grappling with, and list the specific ways these same issues arise in your parenting.

- Establish guidelines and priorities for yourself, and key times to follow them.

- If you have a partner, use a tag-team approach. When one of you is becoming overwhelmed and overreactive, or is withdrawing and becoming underreactive, have a signal system to intervene and take over. Develop this beforehand.

- Have a conference table set aside for negotiations and conflict resolution. Have separate rules for such conferences.

- Establish a feedback system with your partner to help you give and receive observations regarding parenting.

- Involve a family therapist to help monitor your efforts, enrich your family experiences, work through roadblocks, and resolve conflicts.

- Establish all rules and consequences only when you and your partner are calm, rational, and in control. Involve your children in developing the rules as much as possible.

- Work at setting aside time and creating situations to ensure quality time to rebuild and restructure positive relationships.

The main goal is to not do irreversible damage to relationships with your children, spouse, and parents while resolving personal issues and restructuring family convolutions. Families, despite all their difficulties and limitations, are precious. We need their understanding, support, and love. They deserve our care.

Part III

Reclaiming Your Future

Something is still missing. We have faced the challenge of recovery, wrestled with the demons of our past, and now we expect to be rewarded with a sense of completion.

As we surrender the burdens of guilt and shame, we reawaken to the world around and within us. Now we can make tangible plans, carry out projects, and rebuild satisfying relationships—we can experience the true joys of living.

Yet where we expected to find peace, we may find we have become restless. Where we hoped to experience true happiness, that happiness rings hollow. The flavor of our lives has vastly improved, but we are disturbed by a feeling that something remains incomplete. Recovery promised new life, new hope, so what is it we still crave?

The discomfort, the hunger we now feel, is the hunger for growth. It pushes us to take the next step. This time our internal discontent is not a sign of disease, but rather an indication that we have further to go. Our disquiet challenges us to reach further, to let ourselves reach for the selves we were intended to become.

This newly acquired power, resources, and balance place us in a unique position. Through our growth during recovery we have completed the preconditions for a personal evolution.

Life, living, is about more than just being happy. We are born with certain qualities, certain possibilities. To live fully means to fulfill our potential, to satisfy our higher level needs of purpose, autonomy, integrity, and connection with the world around us.

By reclaiming our past and present, we have positioned ourselves for the final task that makes all of the pain and effort worthwhile: we are poised to reclaim our future.

8

Our Original Life Trajectory

We are all born into this world on a mission. Several complications immediately arise, the central one being that we have no idea what our mission entails. Who assigns our mission is equally unclear. Some believe it's God, some feel the universe quietly decides, and a few believe it is a drive inborn in us. We don't even arrive knowing that we are on a mission in the first place. We spend the first part of our journey finding out about the world, its nature and complexity, process, and contents. Then we start finding out what we have to work with, our talents, skills, needs, and strengths. About the time we are old enough to get into serious trouble, we find out how to work with the world.

As time goes on, we begin to see what pieces are still missing, what's wrong, and where the holes are. Finally, a few of us find that some of our talents and skills fill some of those holes. Through our efforts, the universe becomes a little more complete. At that point we have discovered our mission, and we ourselves are more complete. Somehow the needs of the world are met by our meeting our own higher order needs—the inspirations and motivations behind what we do.

Life is funny that way.

Now we are on the brink of breakthrough. We are unfolding in ways previously unthinkable. Each of us, in her or his own way, has traversed a set of steps leading from where we once were toward where we were meant to be. In the course of working through this book, we have:

- assessed the nature and costs of our derailment
- confronted root feelings and recaptured forgotten parts of ourself
- acknowledged and utilized the special gifts our experience has given us

Now we need to redirect our energies back on the proper path for our journey, to see where we are really going.

Needs, Tasks, and Directions

So far in this book we have talked in practical terms about ourselves, our needs, our past experiences, and present remedies. Now it is time to step back a little and look at some of the larger issues, the existential backdrop against which we act out our lives. Now we need to ask the questions that we often dismiss as religion or philosophy: Who *are* we really? What drives us, keeps us going? What are we here for? And how can we be happy?

Those of you who prefer the practical and the active may be tempted to skip this section and move on. I urge you to read it, however. These questions come up again and again in our lives and it helps to have an approach and a context for answering them.

However interesting life may be, it isn't free. You are not owed happiness or peace. Your good works and striving do not have to pay off with some reward. If you have the phenomenal luck to be born, you already have been graced with the greatest reward of all, life itself. If your striving pays off, you have been doubly graced. But while you may not have a right to expect a full and happy life to be given to you, you do have the right to take one.

The original blueprint of your life is your own optimal growth. You were born with certain talents and you have developed some strengths. Your life task consists of using the full potential of your capacities in the situation in which you find yourself. Thus, your life trajectory is the path between your origins and the fulfillment of your potential.

At the root of human existence lie four pervasive conditions which shape our experience of the world and ourselves: separateness, absurdity, finitude, and mortality. These four themes influence our perceptions of life events and the meaning we derive from them. Because these conditions directly affect our fundamental sense of well-being, they present an ultimate and overwhelming threat and we usually experience them indirectly, often unconsciously. For this reason, each serves as the origin of a higher order need or drive which motivates our thinking and our actions. Each need, in turn, shapes a life task which we undertake in our pursuit of well-being, a task which lasts throughout our lifetime and evolves as we do.

Separateness and the task of connecting

Each of us possesses a unique, individual consciousness that separates us from others. Sensing the essential separateness of our existence, we seek to connect with others and with the world around us, to touch with our fingers, our hearts, and our minds. We do this through sharing and communicating life experiences. A host of feelings such as love, hate, loneliness, and empathy guide us in the life task of seeking connection. We achieve connectedness through intimate relations with our family and significant others, affiliation with groups of friends and organizations, and a personal, metaphysical union with the universe and God.

When we fulfill our need for connectedness we feel satisfied and joyful—our relationships are rewarding. When we don't, we experience alienation, isolation, and abandonment. The loneliness we feel resonates with our fundamental separateness and makes us anxious.

Often, to avoid the anxiety and dread of being alone, we settle for the "next best thing": a drink, drug, casual sex, or some other high which provides a temporary, counterfeit experience of peace. For a moment we feel a connection. Unfortunately, these counterfeit experiences only serve to reinforce our isolation and make relationships more difficult to sustain. We don't stretch and develop authentic connections with others, instead we grow more dependent on the drug, the substitute, and it in turn prevents others from connecting with us. Ultimately, addictions and compulsions undermine our higher order need for fulfilling relationships.

Absurdity and the task of finding purpose

As children we grow up in a prefabricated world presented to us by our family and culture. We experience the structure of the world, its moral codes and values as if they were fixed. Even if no one preached to us about how things are or should be, we would still emulate our role models and share this world view. But part of our growth as an individual is the realization that much of this construction is arbitrary. The more we learn to question, the fewer grounds we have for blindly accepting the views (and the ways of viewing) to which we have been accustomed. We realize that many of the assumptions we make about the world are just that—assumptions.

When we challenge the assumed world view, we call into question the value and meaning of any world view. At that point we may sense that much of our life is absurd; that it is based on little more than convention, convenience, or faith. This absurdity is tremendously threatening as it undercuts our basis for making choices and setting directions.

Our grasp of the fundamental absurdity of human existence is often unconscious and intuitive. It expresses itself in our pursuit of meaning and purpose. We need to sense direction in our lives, believe that our efforts will affect the world, and believe that the world itself makes sense. Thus, our task becomes to both fashion a world view in which our actions become meaningful, and find a direction for our lives which makes sense within that world. When we are successful in this task, we experience satisfaction, fulfillment, and derive meaning from living. When we fail in this task we experience meaninglessness, lack of direction, and paralysis. Our lives go on hold, their courses decided by whatever external influences bump into us.

To avoid this existential angst, many settle for counterfeit forms of meaning such as mindless conformity and compulsion. Dependencies provide inauthentic relief—as do the highly rigid and ritualistic institutions such as dogmatic religions, the military, or prison life. Such counterfeit systems of meaning and purpose are ultimately self-sabotaging because they tend to reinforce the underlying sense of purposelessness which they were intended to fix.

Finitude and the task of becoming autonomous

Compared to the vast powers of natural forces and social history, we individuals are finite, small. At some point, we all recognize the limitations of our will. We can always find someone or something more powerful than we are. Because of this, our sense of self cannot lie in controlling the world—we cannot even control ourselves. We can *manage* ourselves, however, and avoid the trap of depending on others for our well-being.

In the face of our limitations, we must ground our self-respect and self-esteem in our autonomy, our capability for self-determination and self-management. If our efforts at satisfying our drive for autonomy are successful we experience true self-worth and can respect others freely. If our efforts at establishing autonomy are thwarted, we suffer from impotence and self-loathing. We may engage in self-destructive behaviors in an effort to gain control over our lives, or we may settle for the counterfeit experience of controlling others. Such abuses of power just create situations which further reinforce our experience of being limited.

Mortality and the task of integration

Ultimately, we are all mortal. While we may hold fast to beliefs about after-life or multiple lives, we have no unimpeachable evidence to demonstrate its existence. Just as the cold war generation grew up knowing that thermonuclear annihilation was never more than a heartbeat away, we are all confronted with death, the ultimate negator of existence, the destroyer of our dreams. Whatever our beliefs about death, the *fact* of death places a horizon upon our projects and constructions. From the perspective of death all our relationships, our actions, and our autonomy are transitory.

What we do is important, but it is equally important that it is we who are doing it. Our mortality makes the degree to which our various endeavors are extensions of ourself critically important. When faced with limited time, we must not waste that time. Death sparks within us a drive toward integrity of self.

The task of integration provides an answer to the nihilism and fragmentation we experience when confronted by death. To the extent we integrate our lives, we can experience ourselves as whole persons able to go forth authentically into a limited and uncertain future. We are able to live the time we have fully. If our efforts to achieve integrity are thwarted, we experience fear and vulnerability. Then we may settle for the counterfeit experiences of workaholism or exercise addiction, religious dogmatism, or other compulsive attempts to avoid fragmentation and depression and to purchase immortality.

These four conditions and their corresponding basic needs—separateness/connection, absurdity/purpose, finitude/autonomy, and mortality/integrity—together provide the building blocks for our identity. The way in which we respond to the task of balancing them shapes the person we become.

Being

At first glance two of these drives seem contradictory. How can one satisfy the need for connectedness and autonomy at the same time? How can we be for others and still be ourselves? This brings up a fundamental aspect of our nature as human beings. We are of the world, which means that part of our nature is to be with the world, with other people. Yet, as beings we are also an object, a separateness, an individual.

But the contradiction is only apparent. Autonomy and connectedness do not stand in an either-or relationship. In fact, these needs are better presented graphically in the Chinese yin-yang symbol of complementarity:

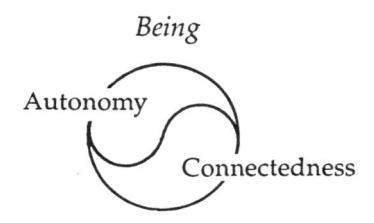

Being

Autonomy

Connectedness

This is an apparent paradox, yet it is only through exploring this paradox that we can become ourselves. Autonomy must be developed hand in hand with connectedness. Autonomy does not mean standing in isolation; in sustained isolation a part of us dies. We can only be truly ourselves within a supportive community, where individuality is balanced by interpersonal contact.

The same is true of our need for connectedness. If we were to attempt to bond with others without concurrently developing our autonomy, we would lose our ability to manage our lives and would lose our own self in the process. Connectedness without a self is not relationship; it is empty dependency.

Thus the question "to be or not to be . . . ?" is not a yes/no question. While it is clear that we can commit suicide by terminating our life, it is less obvious but equally true that we commit partial suicide every moment in which we live in a less than autonomous, less than connected manner. "Being" means being for ourselves and being for others, and so isolation is suicide, just as is dependency.

Doing

We are more than a body with a mind inside. We may see ourselves as objects, continually shaped by the events around us, but we are also an event, part of a process, unfolding through our personal growth and evolution, our relationships and our world involvement. Our identity is more than our being; it is also our actions, our choices, and our decisions. We must rightly see ourselves as actors.

Our actions, if they are to be satisfying and fulfilling, also serve two masters. Just as connectedness and autonomy reflect polar aspects of our essential nature as "being," purpose and integrity reflect a polarity within our essential nature as "doing." And this apparent polarity again hides an interdependence.

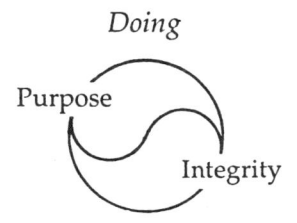

Doing

Purpose

Integrity

The existential question, "to be or not to be . . . ?" here translates into "to do or not to do . . . ?" While, as doers, our acts give structure and purpose to our world, they must also reflect an inner integrity and continuity.

By acting purposefully in the world we try to overcome the basic absurdity of existence. Yet our actions must have integrity, they must be our own. Actions and endeavors not in consonance with our experience and value structures are not grounded in our identity. The meaning we project into the world by such acts is not our own. When we participate in such endeavors we reinforce the very absurdity we are trying to overcome, and our actions are schizoid, separated from ourself.

Similarly, our actions must be grounded in the world. While in order to overcome our own mortality we must act with integrity, our actions cannot be just for ourselves. Our projects must take into account the state of the world and take as their meaning their effects in the world. Cut off from the world our actions are no more than the flailings of a dying person. Our histories, values, and world views can be transcendent—can answer the inevitability of death—only if they generate fruit outside of ourselves.

Being and Doing across the lifespan

Purposeful action takes place at the interface between our connection into the world and our autonomous self, and is grounded in our integrity. Each of the other needs are fulfilled at a similar interface between inner and outer, personal and interpersonal. Our development as a whole person can only take place through balanced, concurrent achievement of each task across our lifetime. Each of the tasks of connection, purpose, autonomy, and integrity takes place at each of our developmental stages and the pains and anguish, joys and fulfillment of each stage of life are related to the appropriate satisfaction of these needs.

In the same way, the inevitable setbacks and losses, trials and traumas of life are related to each of our four basic conditions. They affect the completion of each task at each life-stage. Understanding the effects of learning experiences and life choices on our basic needs and tasks gives us direction for understanding and reclaiming the future.

Reconnection and Transformation

If in the living of your life you have encountered less than optimal conditions, such as traumas and resulting dependencies, you have likely fallen considerably short of your original life trajectory. The difference between the life you are now leading and the life you were created to lead is the future you must reclaim.

The effort and sacrifice it takes is the price you must pay for the gift of a full and complete life.

Reconnecting with your original life trajectory is the first step in reclaiming your future. Because it is difficult to remember something so early and basic, the following exercises may help:

- Begin by recalling as much of your early childhood as possible. Break out any family photo albums or memorabilia you may have. Look for messages implicit in the pictures regarding the love and respect that you received.

- Talk to people who knew your family. Ask them about the visions and dreams they had for you.

- Look at any artwork and writing you may have done. What sort of dreams do they reflect?

- Look for your own early memories about your direction. Use some of the writing exercises in earlier chapters to help tap these.

- Use a relaxation protocol to access early memories or deep feelings that may be otherwise difficult to reach. Purchase a commercial relaxation tape, look over the ideas in Chapter Four, or make an audio tape for yourself as outlined below.

When you make your own tape, write out a script and record yourself reading it. Speak slowly and calmly, pausing a moment between each direction or suggestion. When you are ready to relax, find a comfortable place where you will not be disturbed. Sit or lie down and turn on the tape. Modify the model script to fit your needs, substituting images to which you respond best, and adding specific suggestions you want to work with:

> "You are about to become very relaxed. If you feel particular points of tension in your body, allow them to relax as you take three deep breaths. Take in the fresh air through your nose and allow it to release through your mouth. Let yourself relax as you breathe. Feel the tension leaving you as you exhale.
>
> "Focus your attention on the very top of your head. Notice any tension. Squeeze all of the muscles of your head, forehead, and face. Hold the squeeze (pause), now release and relax those muscles fully. Do it again (pause). Feel all of the muscles around the top of your head becoming warm and relaxed."

In the script, move down from major muscle group to major muscle group, head to feet, down the entire body. Squeeze and relax each muscle group twice.

> "Feel the warmth and relaxation spreading throughout your body; feel the warmth and heaviness. Now imagine yourself in a very safe place; some place that has been a comfort to you in the past, or could be in the future. You are walking through this special place; notice the sights and sounds. Following the path you somehow find yourself in a garden. There are three seats there in the garden, and you choose one. As you

sit down, you sink into a far deeper state of relaxation than you were before, or perhaps than you have ever been before.

"Rest . . . every minute you spend in this garden rests you more deeply than a thirty-minute nap. Look around and enjoy the freshness and timelessness of your inner sanctuary garden. Spend some time creating this special place which you will always have with you. Then gradually becoming more aware of your feelings, you relax further, losing sense of time."

At this point any number of suggestions can be given, including some for imagining your original life trajectory. After these suggestions, or a several-minute pause for deep relaxation, the script can be closed with the following:

"It is time to return. Note once more the details of the garden and the transformations which have occurred here. Now take your leave and stand up, returning up the path, back to your present. Clap your hands once, assisting yourself to become fully awake, feeling strong, good, relaxed, and alive!"

The following suggestions for recalling your original life trajectory may be incorporated into your relaxation tape as indicated above:

"Review in your mind's eye your trials through _____ (your disease). (Pause for a minute or so between each sentence.) Move back in time to the painful experiences that led to _____ (your disease). Move back still further, to a time before your pain—a time when the world was fresh and bursting with possibilities and opportunities. See yourself at that time, sitting with the future opening before you. Feel the excitement within! See your future take the form of a huge golden arch, reaching up from where you sit to far, far overhead, disappearing into the sky. Feel yourself start to rise up with that golden arch, riding it up through the sky. See your life unfolding again, encountering each difficult moment and turning each into the most wonderful experience. Recreate and relive each event with a growing, healing, perfect new outcome. Every event is lived the right way. Live your life again the way it was meant to be lived! (Pause several minutes to allow processing.) Feel yourself bathed in a golden light."

In the last chapter we will look again at some of the dysfunctions and traumas you have faced in your life—and perhaps worked on in this book. We will see how they can give you clues to the tasks that lie ahead for you and the themes that will be dominant in your transformation, for that is what you are embarked on now. Reclaiming your future is nothing less than a transformation—a complete shedding of your old self and old life, the surrender of the chrysalis and the emergence of the butterfly.

9

A Pilgrim's Progress

We are all pilgrims, each on her or his journey to the sacred place. Our path leads toward fulfillment of our needs and the needs of the world. Through our derailment from this trajectory we lived half-lives of unfulfilled promise. Our difficulties, on the other hand, have provided gifts of experience, strengthening, and resources. Now we can recreate a purposeful future.

Derailment and the Half-Lived Life

After recovery we may live life too carefully for our own good. Our background makes us reluctant to involve ourselves or make large commitments to others. The constricted post-trauma, post-dependent lifestyle does not invest in the future in an expansive way. To be open to the future, or even to the present, requires belief that the world can be trusted. But past hurt and personal dependencies have conditioned us to expect the worst from the world and ourselves, to fear the unknown, and to live a life of denial, distortion, minimization, selective perception, and careful response. We limit ourselves to half-lived lives.

Derailed from our original life trajectory, we find our futures constrained by encrustations from the past. We are like coral polyps building unbendable life patterns which determine and direct our future. Our limited and limiting decisions fix conditions that could be otherwise flexible. The longer we live, the more we limit and define our options. Our encrustations can include:

- traits and dispositions destined by heredity and reinforced by the consequences of our decisions
- expectations of the world formed by our early background
- attitudes, perspectives, and conceptions of the world based upon key experiences, including traumatic events

These encrustations maintain our derailment from our original trajectory. Can they be overcome? Maybe. With intentional effort of the kind begun in the first two parts of this book our conceptions and perceptions can be relearned, and perspectives thus altered; attitudes and expectations can be transformed; response and habit patterns can be broken and reshaped; even physical and neurological conditions can be modified and treated.

Derailment from our original trajectory affects the fulfilling of our higher order needs differently. To the extent the need for connectedness is compromised, for instance, we may become isolated from significant others, groups, and from the world in general. Thwarting the need for purpose can result in a life of meaninglessness and absurdity. If our needs for autonomy and integrity go unmet, the result can be dependency and self-loathing. Practically speaking, key areas in our life suffer when our higher order needs are unmet. Our emotional development, career, relationships, and spirituality are all likely to fall victim.

The post-traumatic, dependent life is one of chronic underproductivity, and the promise of full recovery is an invitation to commitment, to full performance. This can be terribly frightening for the chronic underproducer. It is experienced as a loss of control, a complete vulnerability. It feels like being sucked into a vortex, a whirlpool dragging one down—though really it is pulling us up!

The second task in reclaiming your future entails assessing the cost of trauma and dependency in terms of your development. Consider ways in which your original trajectory was derailed:

- Draw a time line on a large piece of paper contrasting your original trajectory with your present development. Indicate on the line when early traumas or later dependencies occurred.

- Think about your current state of derailment. How have you fallen short of your original potential for connectedness, purpose, autonomy, and integrity?

- Draw a chart indicating how your trajectory in each of the above goals has affected your emotional development, career path, relationships, and spiritual growth.

Lost Feelings, Lost Selves

Our distortions, minimizations, denial, selectivity, and reaction patterns can be altered—but only if they are no longer needed. They were necessary because they served deep-seated root feelings. Exploring and redirecting these feelings is necessary for the eventual breaking of the limiting encrustations of the past.

We have a rich array of feelings, reactions, impulses, desires, and perceptions which we force out of our consciousness in order to make ourselves more acceptable to others or more manageable for ourselves.

Some of these we exile from our consciousness because we associate them with negative experiences or persons we fear. Others we exile because we outgrow them. Still others presented a social liability at a particular stage of our development, and we still have not reclaimed them. They now represent a treasure trove of energy and strength, and can include cherished dreams, ideas, and spiritual ideals which were given up through the fears, disillusionment, and constriction of trauma and addiction.

Much of the energy we have been taught to suppress through our socialization or trauma lies within us in a chaotic, unfocused state. This energy works against us in two ways. Because it has no outlet it infects our will, distorting our efforts and causing us to sabotage ourselves. Secondly, because we must put energy into controlling it, it robs us of the energy we need to pursue our various endeavors.

These feelings and reaction patterns tend to cluster into complexes, or "selves." One such complex might be a "self" we experienced at five years of age, with all its attendant ways of looking at and responding to the world. Another might be a "parental self," or the collection of perceptions and responses we learned by identifying with our parents. A third might be our "victim self" who still suffers because of an earlier trauma. Some of this multiplicity of selves is part of our normal, daily life. Some is more hidden, even from us. We are driven both by those response sets we are aware of, and those we are not.

Sometimes a particularly strong reaction complex will develop to where it takes over more and more of our energy, operating quite close to the surface of our consciousness so that we almost feel its presence, a "shadow" self.

Two sources of root reactions are our personal experience and the basic needs themselves. Frightening or confusing experiences, for example, can create fear reactions that can be extremely uncomfortable. The mind will then seek to avoid them. Similarly, experiences during childhood, or during fits of dependency, can leave deep-seated feelings of inadequacy and low self-worth and cause us to avoid similar situations. The basic needs, on the other hand, can create root reactions just through our awareness of them. Our need for connection, for instance, can create loneliness and abandonment.

Often, deep-seated feelings lying hidden within us cause much of our unpredictable, confusing, or self-limiting behavior. Margaret's drive to lose herself in a frenzy of eating was motivated by a deep need to do something purposeful in the world. This conflicted with her fear of violating early family role relationships in which she was the nonachiever. She avoided the pain of her sister's loss by maintaining the family myth of her own mediocrity. The energy to become involved in something bigger than herself, however, took the self-abusive form of bingeing. Thus her rebellious compulsion was a substitute for a life involvement of real purpose and autonomy.

Because she came to grips with the loss and fears of abandonment, Margaret is no longer plagued by the impulse to binge. Once she was able to let go of her fear and grieve her pain, a tremendous energy was released into her life.

Discovering and confronting these deep-seated reactions not only helps us become aware of our hidden motives, but also gives us a means to orchestrate a richer, more satisfying life. By acknowledging our shadow selves, we can reconcile our various needs and drives, and we tap a tremendous inner resource. Moreover, the shadow selves we have been fighting often hold much of the higher power we need to draw on when we begin to respond to our higher order needs.

Here are some ways to begin identifying hidden feelings, thoughts, and motives:

- Go within, through meditation, prayer, artwork, or discussion with someone helpful, and seek that of which you are the most afraid, most ashamed.
- Use visualizations or self-hypnosis to help you get in touch with feelings and memories.
- Talk to people who know you well, and who have known you over time. Get their observations and perceptions.
- Keep a dream log.
- Keep notes regarding your reactions to themes in movies, books, or television.
- Talk to and do dreamwork with a counselor or licensed clinical hypnotherapist.
- Use the relaxation protocol outlined in the last chapter to enlist the aid of that part of you that monitors both your surface, social self, and the deeper parts within.

Inner Work

Psychotherapist Courtney Peterson created a wonderful metaphor for the life journey. He likened each of us to a bus, driving down the road of life. The bus has a driver and a conductor, and is filled with passengers. Some of the passengers ride toward the front of the bus, conferring among themselves and offering suggestions to the driver. Every now and then one of these passengers takes over driving. Toward the back of the bus sit those passengers who have little input into setting the course or managing the trip. Some of them are passive, and some are rebellious, creating disturbances to gain attention and slow things down. As the bus rumbles along, destinations must be set, guides consulted, laws complied with, obstacles avoided, equipment maintained, breakdowns repaired, and other traffic negotiated.

Who is riding on this bus? Peterson likens the driver to our "social self," which deals with the world and attempts to pilot this juggernaut on its proper course. Each of the passengers is one of the subpersonalities that we have bound together to make up who we have become. They are the different perspectives from which we have viewed the world, the sets of responses we have retained from different stages of our lives and impressions of people with whom we have identified. They include the child we were at five, our parents, perhaps a significant teacher, unique experiences, hurts, needs. Now they are parts of us, sometimes central, sometimes peripheral. We used to, still can, and sometimes cannot avoid "getting into" each, seeing and reacting to the world from that perspective.

A central character on the bus is the conductor, who plays a mediating role between passengers and driver, and plays a special role in setting the course and keeping perspective. In literary and mythological traditions, this is the wise old man or woman, the oracle, the priest, the mystic.

By getting in touch with these response-complexes within ourselves we can access feelings, perceptions, memories, and resources which are often otherwise dormant.

The following exercise helps identify some of the more prominent passengers on our bus and on our journey:

Get a large piece of paper. Draw the outline of a large bus, making sure you include at least eight to ten windows. Now draw the driver. Make this one resemble yourself as much as possible. Then work at identifying and drawing the major players in your inner group. Don't be afraid to exaggerate characters, or use animals or symbols when they better express the energy behind the character. If you suspect a particular character's existence but have no definition yet, draw an empty box. You can return later and fill in the blanks.

Keep this drawing and add to it as your inner awareness increases. Modify it with road signs, obstacles, and crossroads, adding each character's input regarding decisions with which the driver is faced.

Once you begin to get in touch with root feelings, reactions, and "selves" within, spend some time thinking about where they came from. Try associating them with the experiences you dealt with in Chapters Five, Six, and Seven. Review those chapters with this perspective in mind. In particular, review the comments in Chapter Five concerning taking care of yourself during times of self-examination.

Consulting your inner oracle

The inner guide, or oracle, is a source of wisdom. Direct consultation opens communication which can be very fruitful. Further, the oracle can serve as an intermediary in your attempts to make contact with other inner selves. Incorporate the following passages into the relaxation tape you were asked to make in Chapter Eight.

> "Sitting in one of the seats in your garden, you await the arrival of someone very special. You are calm and confident, knowing that this special person is your inner oracle, a wise person who sees beyond the present, past, and future. You may be surprised at the form this person takes.
>
> "When the oracle has appeared, ask what he or she wants to be called. If you are feeling uncomfortable, you might ask the oracle why. Feel free to ask the oracle any question you wish. Consider asking about the course you are presently following. Be open to suggestion. Ask about ways in which you may be sabotaging yourself. Ask if there are realities or obligations which you are ignoring in your drive for meeting your goals."

Make contact with other selves within

Use the following protocol for establishing contact and maintaining a working relationship with otherwise estranged parts of yourself. Incorporate the following questions into your relaxation protocol.

Ask the inner oracle to join you in your sacred garden, and to sit down in one of the other seats. Ask the oracle to help you contact the person within who is causing the most derailment. Follow the oracle's direction.

When the shadow self arrives, whatever its form, invite it to sit in the third seat. Ask its name, its origin, and its function within your inner group. Ask the following:

- Why are you resisting me?
- What is your purpose?
- What is the deep feeling or knowledge you are protecting?
- What protections or assurances do you need in order to accomplish your mission?
- What can I do differently to help you?
- What resources do you have to offer me?
- How can I utilize them for our mutual benefit?

Make a pact with the inner self to protect each other, and work toward each other's needs.

Reactions that were once forbidden may turn out to be valuable reservoirs of revitalizing power. The process of going within can transform wasted energy into meeting higher order needs. Even negative, anti-social energy may be diverted to positive ends. In any case, the energy that has been spent in denying and suppressing these shadow selves can be redirected toward the future.

Trading Pain for the Gifts of Experience

Through recovery we learn that we can stabilize the chaos in our lives and regain manageability. This is a good lesson for the future; we know that just as we will always live with the risk of relapse, we do have the proven power to regain stability. We have gained much more, however, our derailment provides us with an invaluable cutting edge.

Our cultural background is full of images of the redemptive power of adversity. Literature and mythology shows how we can be tested by fire, tempered by the crucible of defeat, and challenged to respond heroically. If we emerge triumphant we can become the wise woman or man giving guidance to the next generation of seekers and heroes.

Many people go through life taking their blessings for granted, impatient with challenges, defeated by adversity, lost in a seemingly endless round of daily struggles. They are complacent with their lives and live far below their capacity. For those who need to be shaken from their slumber, catastrophe can be a blessing.

Crisis shakes the bonds of complacency and resistance. Trauma, beyond its obvious cost, deepens the resonance of our experience, teaches us compassion, and infuses our lives with a need for purpose.

Through events which threaten our personal status quo we can learn that the good life is not a reward for right action but rather a priceless gift with which we have been already graced. Trauma can sensitize us to the fragility and importance of our lives. Compulsions and addictions can awaken us to our need for authentic purpose and connection. Recovery is more than restabilization, more than just cutting losses. Recovery can prepare us to utilize the gifts of our experience to rechannel our lives in ways previously impossible.

When we were dysfunctional we felt that the isolation, dependency, absurdity, and self-loathing of our lives was permanent. Through our struggles to overcome the bonds of dependency, we empowered ourselves with self-awareness, knowledge, perspective, skills, and resources. "Bottoming out" had its rewards: isolation showed us our need for connectedness, absurdity for purpose; dependency created hunger for autonomy, and self-loathing made us look for integrity.

You can now cash in on your gifts of experience, trading pain for advantage. Spend some time with pencil and paper assessing what you have received as a result of your recovery. If you have been keeping a notebook or journal from prior exercises, add to that. In a page or so for each, assess what you have learned and become as a result of your addictions and recovery. Also:

- Review this section, circling or writing down specific points that apply to you.

- Look for the higher directions you have set as a result of these experiences. See those directions as a reflection of your growing capacity.

- Determine how those assets could be applied to your journey toward becoming yourself.

- Appreciate how difficult attaining your projects would be without these hard-won gifts. What goals, projects, growth are now possible?

- Develop an attitude of gratitude for your experiences, your life. How could you possibly repay the universe for your gifts? What do you owe?

- Thinking about how long your evolution has taken, consider striking the following bargain with the universe, that it will grant you all the time and all the experiences you need, if in turn you agree to be fully yourself.

♦ ♦ ♦

Barbara *has been recovering from an eating disorder for five years. She has developed a deeper sense of herself and has strengthened her relationships. Now she is ready to do more.*

The dinner dishes were cleaned up, the homework was finished, and the children were in bed. Barbara and Art were decompressing at the kitchen table before deciding what to do with what was left of the evening, and had fallen into conversation.

"You know, Art, I've watched you do your work and make job changes. We've talked about the externals like salary, benefits, stresses, and that sort of thing. We've even talked about whether it was what you wanted to do. But we've never shared . . . I've never asked what everything has meant to you."

"I know," he replied, a little uncomfortably. "It never seemed to come up. Things are different now. I hope we can."

"You seem to know where you are going. You know that's what I'm trying to figure out for myself. How did you ever find your sense of direction?" Her adamant tone left no doubt that she expected a thoughtful answer.

Art took a deep breath and let it out slowly. "When I was a kid I went through ten or twenty ideas of 'what I was gonna be when I grew up.' But I always thought that by the time I grew up I would know. The path would be clear. By the time I turned thirty-five I had been several of them and was still wondering. I never wanted to let you know how uncertain I was because it seemed that my job was to provide security. Besides, I thought at the time that your worry wouldn't help. I'm learning differently. At forty-five, I feel that I am finally on the right track, even though I have learned to stay open to what the future might bring."

"You mean you had several false starts? I always thought you were just changing jobs to make more money," interrupted Barbara.

"Not exactly. Each time I learned something new and had more to bring to the next one."

Barbara was not satisfied. "So you've given up finding the right niche, the right career?"

"Hardly," Art answered. "Each time I come closer, and lately I've been learning fast." He sipped his coffee and continued. "I have some sense of what my strengths are, and a lot more understanding about how I can use them. It's becoming clearer and clearer to me that I must use my talents and energies in service to others. I'm doing this at a level I never conceived of when I was twenty-five, and I'm excited about what the next twenty years will bring."

Barbara was thoughtful. "Does everyone take this long to figure out what his or her purpose is?"

"Yes and no," laughed Art. "I would hope that other people's visions are also limited by inexperience, as mine were. But some people do seem to have a better sense of themselves a lot earlier than I did. Take my sister, for example. From the time she was fourteen she was clear that what she wanted to do was music. She even picked out the conservatory at which she would study. There were a few twists and turns along the way, but her life was a pretty consistent unfolding of her career. She's nearly forty-three now, and has joy and satisfaction from her work. She's happy!"

"That certainly didn't happen to me," Barbara thought out loud.

Art laughed. "It certainly would be easier. But I think diversity can bring depth and breadth. I like to believe that I can do what I do now because of diversity, not in spite of it."

Barbara stood up and stretched. She paced back and forth, as if trying to walk off her agitation. Finally her question surfaced. "But how can you keep from getting hopelessly sidetracked? Or if you're stuck, how do you get back on track with your life? What if you find yourself in the middle of your life stuck in a rut and hardly even knowing who you are?" Her question was obviously deeply personal.

"I don't know, Barb," said Art, feeling compassion for her pain. "To begin with, I'm not all that clear where the 'middle' of a life is. Sometimes I feel as if mine has just begun. And if my experiences have been preparing me for this moment, then it would seem that I couldn't have my future without my past. And if I do have a purpose, who's to say I'm ready to fulfill it yet? Maybe I still need 'ripening.'"

"Yes," interjected Barbara, "but how do I know what to do next? What I may have done so far may have been in preparation for something, but I need to know how to proceed right now!"

"Barbara," replied Art, "you have to trust that you yourself will know. I think you have to open yourself to what the world is telling you, do what really feels right. Follow the path of satisfaction—not pleasure, not fun in the sense of immediate gratification, satisfaction. You have to do what is fulfilling. Trust that at some level, you can be satisfied only by doing what is right for you."

♦ ♦ ♦

Although it was late, Barbara wasn't ready for sleep. Too many unanswered questions had been raised. Turmoil kept her from relaxing, and Barbara decided to walk it off.

For the first several blocks she mulled over her conversation with Art. How wonderful to have someone with whom she could share this adventure. And to be married to him! But where was it all going? In a way it was frightening to realize that her options were open.

She remembered an image she had several days earlier at a workshop. She had been in a state of deep relaxation when the leader had suggested they envision their problem in some tangible form on a seat. Barbara had surprised herself by imaging great bags of food hanging from a saddle on the back of a horse. Saying good-bye to this would be easy.

At that point she noticed that the saddle itself was not empty. In it was strapped an empty body brace, the type that supports people with disabilities from their knees to their shoulders. She had been struck at the time with the dual role of such a contraption; while it provided support for a body that could not sit up unattended, it also restricted motion. While Barbara's eating disorder had provided her needed support, it also kept her from getting to where she needed to be.

But where did she need to be? When she was growing up, she had felt that she was very special, destined for important things. Her subsequent life choices gradually obscured her vision. Her eating disorder compounded her paralysis. But like a disabled person who relies upon the constraints of the brace for support, Barbara was terrified when the restraints were removed. The future seemed unbounded, chaotic, and threatening. She longed for a map, or even a compass. How do I know, she asked herself, if I can make the changes that lie ahead?

As she walked by the convenience store, Barbara was reminded of the despair she once battled. Those were difficult times, she mused. Yet she had grown so much since then. While she was no longer the young girl with unlimited time and few obligations, she now had some hard-won strengths, skills, and experience. Whatever goal she finally set, she was confident she now had considerable resources.

The night air seemed alive. Insect sounds, the smell of night-blooming jasmine, and the sounds of life coming from the houses she passed mixed together in a heady blend. The stars seemed especially alive tonight.

It all seemed to be linked together. It was just too much of a stretch to assume that the recent events, her life, the trees, and stars were not part of a pattern. Looking both ways as she crossed the street, Barbara opened herself a little more. I just have to trust that I am a part of this pattern, she thought.

She was walking faster, now. As she walked, Barbara felt for the pattern inside. She knew it was there even if she hadn't sorted out the details. As she passed under a streetlight on that warm, spring night, she was lost, immersed in the connectedness and importance of it all.

Recapturing Your Pilgrim Soul

To recapture our pilgrimage we must take bold steps forward. The light of the world is our own light. We must let go of our self-limitations, cease holding back, and turn toward that light. Our journey, our search, our mission in the world awaits. Our choice is between complacency and purpose, half-life and living fully. If we are to create ourselves fully, we must look both inward and outward for inspiration, and we must allow our talents, power, and individuality to celebrate this transformation. Three steps begin this journey:

Let go of your fear, distrust, and self-deprecation

Distrust of yourself and of the world underlie your reluctance to take your journey seriously. If you recognize that your attitudes and feelings are constricted, you can become intentionally expansive. By extending yourself incrementally, you learn to take risks that matter. By realizing your strength, you can allow yourself to deepen your connection into the world. Acknowledging your power, you can dare autonomy. Trusting your vision, you can choose a direction for your life. As your strength increases through the purpose and integrity of your action, take larger steps toward the world:

- Suspend belief in your flaws.
- Act on the assumption that things work out for the best.
- Look for the long-range good, the silver lining.
- Talk gently to yourself; say the things you would say to your child.
- Using your relaxation protocol, visualize doing the things of which you are afraid. Teach yourself to relax in the face of such images.
- Do the things you fear in small doses, relaxing in between and celebrating your successes.

Let go of your blind pursuit of status, glitz, and instant gratification

We are conditioned by social forces around us to unquestioningly pursue the external marks of success. We are beguiled by the shine, the things, the lies. As long as you are dependent upon the external symbols defined by others as indicators of success and substance, you are destined to suffer; a pawn for someone else's gratification. On the other hand, you don't have to abandon your responsibilities for providing security for your family, assistance for your friends, and contributing to your community.

- Look for the important, not the most obvious.
- Be aware of the way in which "sellers" and "persuaders" of all sorts bid for your attention.
- Learn to keep your long-range purpose and goals close to your heart.

- Make your decisions intentional; avoid reflexive choosing.
- When confronted by temptation, ask, "How much am I willing to sacrifice for this?"
- Find ways to balance your inner and outer needs.

Be open to your inner compass, Higher Power, and heart

Each of us has a voice within that acts as an inner compass, keeping us on course through all of our dilemmas and decisions. In the midst of your trauma and addiction the voice of the inner oracle competed with many others—voices of fear, anger, and betrayal. But when you regained stability and began your healing, you began to discern your inner direction again. This voice is heard in subtle form, in quiet truths, in dreams and visions, in the midst of activity, and through your growing awareness. You see it outside of yourself in books, friends, and those whom you admire. You see it reflected in the faces and actions of those whom you have touched.

- Become sensitized to the ways in which the inner oracle speaks softly.
- Use appropriate strategies from Chapter Eight as well as from the preceding sections in this chapter to deepen your contact with the inner oracle.
- Use the oracle protocol on page 176–177 in order to communicate directly with the inner oracle. Ask specific questions about the oracle's vision of your direction and purpose, and how to get there.
- Once you have established direct contact with the

oracle, use empty chair dialogue to reinforce and strengthen your communication.

- Visualize yourself from the perspective of the oracle, seeing yourself confronting different situations. Look into the future, seeing the results of those decisions.

- Strengthen contact with the lost parts of yourself, remaining alert for the enriching aspects, redirecting and incorporating the destructive aspects.

Follow your joy, your satisfaction, your love

In fashioning how you spend your days, choose your work and play, your taking and giving, so that your actions become an expression and extension of your deeper self. In making life choices, use your inner compass in conjunction with your experience. Feedback is a gift; read the results of your past choices as a means of informing your next decision. Follow your reactions, your sense of joy, satisfaction, and love, which are the fruits of the paths you choose.

How do you know when you are on your right trajectory? As a consultant to the corporate world, Marsha Sinetar studied the ways in which self-actualizing people approached their work. She reports in her book *Do What You Love, the Money Will Follow* that self-actualizing people treat their work as play, in which they can be more self-aware and present, focusing their "concentrative/creative" abilities. Work becomes a personal calling, an honoring of the life force. The self-actualizing person allows her- or himself to be linked up to others, while exercising personal strengths and talents. Thus, weaknesses are served by the connection with a larger force. Finally, Sinetar points out how work becomes an avenue for the development and expansion of their emerging positive aspects. While the workaholic approaches work to avoid both problems and self, the self-actualizing person's preoccupation with his or her work flows from self-expression and emergence.

Sinetar's observations hold not only for the world of work but for each of our other life endeavors as well. Our pilgrimage takes us through emotional, spiritual, and interpersonal domains as well as through endeavors in the world. Each of these endeavors can become an avenue of unfolding purpose and integrity, connectedness and autonomy, just as our work can. We can learn through our relationships, both friendship and love, how to attain connectedness without sacrificing autonomy. We can learn through our spirituality to achieve our purposes without losing integrity. As these seeming opposites become manifested and orchestrated in our endeavors, we ourselves come closer to realizing our potential.

When we can play, dance, become absorbed, and lose ourselves in our relationships, spiritual life, housecleaning, and communities, we are self-actualizing. When we manifest our purpose, connectedness, integrity, and autonomy in our journey, we are on the right trajectory. When our life has become the encompassing adventure it was meant to be, when the process of our personal emergence mends a tear in the fabric of the universe, we have reclaimed and are becoming our future.

Afterword

Sherry Hoyt's story is yours and mine. We did not have to visit the battlefields of Vietnam or become addicted to alcohol and destructive relationships to experience hurt and loss. We are vulnerable and we are always tempted by dependency. Despite its being true, Sherry's story is a parable for our time.

Like Sherry, we convulsively lurch from one diversion to another in a vain attempt to fill the haunting emptiness caused by our very humanness. The inevitable losses, traumas, and disturbed relationships we endure gain their power over us because they remind us of our limitations. Where satisfaction of our higher order need is thwarted by our inability to accommodate harsh experiences, we settle for counterfeit satisfactions. Our various dependencies serve as constant diversion from our wounds of the spirit.

On the battlefield Sherry had to learn to insulate herself from the men she served. Attachments brought her continual pain, as her patients either died or left for home. Having her own bedrock condition of separateness constantly underscored under conditions of adversity, she learned to isolate herself. Her relationships became convulsive; she threw herself into them compulsively, only to sabotage real intimacy. She chose partners who were unlikely to demand real relationship.

As a result of her recovery work, Sherry was able to move ahead with the more fundamental task of establishing relationships in which her autonomy was not compromised, and through which she could realize herself. Releasing her fears of hurt and abandonment meant that she could begin exploring authentic connections.

Following battle, Sherry's hunger for purpose was thwarted by her fear that idealism would again lead to crushing disillusionment. She created a career within the military that was predictable, useful, and safe. She liked the romantic image of military life, but it was symbolic rather than real for her. It did not provide the sense of mission she sought. While she underwent the ups and downs of normal career development, Sherry's work lacked passionate commitment. Once into recovery Sherry began to come to grips with issues of meaning and purpose. Changing into a civilian role, advocating the interests and serving the needs of service families began the transition.

Now, with her life stabilized and her demons undergoing exorcism, Sherry is redefining and enriching her original life trajectory. What she once longed to be, she is becoming. She is rediscovering and expressing parts of herself which she spent years covering up and protecting. Yet in that long process she has become more than she had ever imagined, with strengths and resources previously unknown.

Sherry is in the middle of reclaiming her future. She is becoming the person she once dreamed of being—and gave up. Nothing is guaranteed in her process, or in yours. There is no summit, no graduation, no point of arrival to mark success. Ask Sherry if her life is better now than a year or so ago, and she will flash a relieved smile and answer "You bet!" Ask her about her future and she will smile again: "Who knows?"

Pain's Promise

At first glance it is a long way from the chaos of addiction or compulsion to the dignity, meaning, and focus of a life of passionate commitment. Measured in the sweat and tears of recovery it seems like a lifetime. Yet it is not all that far. Problem behavior is optimal behavior gone awry. Dependencies are simply perversions of the highest, most intense spiritual absorption. Addicts are merely fallen monks. Compulsives, the overconcerned. Find the purpose, the mission in your life, and your limitations will transform into your strengths. Your wounds will become your inspiration.

Share the struggles and triumphs of your journey. Honor the journeys of those around you. Let those whom you love in on your adventures, and stay connected to theirs.

If you get a chance, write down your comments, suggestions, or better yet, the story of your experiences with this book, and send them to me in care of

Hunter House Publishers
P.O. Box 2914
Alameda, California 94501-0914

I can't promise a personal answer, but I will read your message and I'll try to respond.

Ken Johnson
Claremont, California
1992

Resources

The main resources for dealing with overwhelming behavior problems are Twelve-Step programs in your area. Most are free, effective, and available. Some, such as Alcoholics Anonymous, Narcotics Anonymous, and Overeaters Anonymous, are problem-specific. Others such as Overcomers Anonymous are open to anyone, irrespective of the nature of their compulsive problem. The best way to find the one appropriate for you is to look in the white pages of the telephone book. Look under the heading that fits your problem, although the people at the AA Central Office usually know about the other programs and can direct you to them.

Confide in those family members you have found trustworthy in the past. Look to counselors, ministers, and pastors as possible resources for you. Ask people you know who are in recovery for people they have found to be helpful.

In addition, look for a recovery section in your local book-store, or look for a bookstore specializing in recovery literature. Continue your reading and work on recovery issues in your life.

The following hotlines provide information, referrals, and sometimes crisis intervention by telephone. The numbers are all toll free and the name of the organization reflects its special concern.

AIDS ALL Prevention Center	1-800-322-8911
AIDS Hotline	1-800-551-2728
Alcohol 24-Hour Helpline	1-800-252-6465
BASH (Bulimia Anorexia Self-Help)	1-800-227-4785
Child Help National Child Abuse Hotline	1-800-422-4453
Cocaine Hotline	1-800-262-2462

Covenant House   1-800-999-9999
Eating Disorder Hotline   1-800-233-5450
Food Addiction Hotline   1-800-872-0088
National Child Abuse   1-800-422-4453
National Council of Compulsive Gambling
                                    1-800-552-4700
National Institute on Drug Abuse   1-800-662-4357
STD Hotline   1-800-227-8922

The following Twelve-Steps Anonymous groups have meetings in various communities nationwide. To find a meeting in your area look in the white pages of the telephone directory or call a local hospital or police department.

Adult Children Anonymous
Adult Children of Alcoholics
Alcoholics Anonymous
Alanon (families of alcoholics)
Alateen (teenagers)
Alatot
Bulimics/Anorexics Anonymous
Child Abusers Anonymous
Cocaine Anonymous
Codependents of Sex Addicts
Families Anonymous (families of drug users)
Narcotics Anonymous
Overeaters Anonymous
Overcomers Anonymous
Parents Anonymous (abusing parents, abused children)
Pills Anonymous
Sex Addicts Anonymous
Sexaholics Anonymous
Sex and Love Addicts Anonymous
Shoplifters Anonymous
Smokers Anonymous
Spenders Anonymous

The following organizations can also provide information on the areas of their interest. Write or call and ask them for what you need.

Adult Children of Alcoholics
Central Service Board
P.O. Box 35623
Los Angeles, CA 90035   Tel. (213) 464-4423

Al-Anon Family Group Headquarters
1372 Broadway
New York, NY 10018-0862   Tel. (212) 302-7240

Alateen
1372 Broadway
New York, NY 10018-0862   Tel. (212) 302-7240

Alcoholics Anonymous (A.A.)
General Service Office
P.O. Box 459
Grand Central Station
New York, NY 10163   Tel. (212) 686-1100

American Council on Alcoholism
8501 LaSalle Road, Suite 301
Towson, MD 21204   Tel. (301) 296-5555

American Council for Drug Education
204 Monroe Street
Rockville, MD 20850   Tel. (301) 294-0600

ALMACA: Association of Labor Management Administrators
    and Consultants on Alcoholism, Inc.
1800 N. Kent Street, Suite 907
Arlington, VA 22209   Tel. (703) 522-6272

AMSAODD: American Medical Society on Alcoholism and
    Other Drug Dependencies
12 West 21st Street, 7th Floor
New York, NY 10010   Tel. (212) 206-6770

Chemical People Project/WQED-TV
4802 Fifth Avenue
Pittsburgh, PA 15213   Tel. (412) 622-1491

COAF: Children of Alcoholics Foundation, Inc.
200 Park Avenue, 31st Floor
New York, NY 10166   Tel. (212) 351-2680

Emotions Anonymous
P.O. Box 4245
St. Paul, MN 55104　　　　　　　Tel. (612) 647-9712

Families Anonymous
World Service Office
P.O. Box 528
Van Nuys, CA 91408　　　　　　Tel. (818) 989-7841

Families in Action Drug Information Center
3845 N. Druid Hills Road, Suite 300
Decatur, GA 30033　　　　　　　Tel. (404) 325-5799

Gamblers Anonymous
P.O. Box 17173
Los Angeles, CA 90017　　　　　Tel. (213) 386-8789

The Grief Recovery Institute
8306 Wilshire Boulevard, Suite 21-A
Beverly Hills, CA 90211　　　　　Tel. 1-800-445-4808

Hazelden Foundation
Box 11
Center City, MN 55012　　　　　Tel. 1-800-328-9000

ICAA: American International Council on Alcohol and
　　　Addiction
P.O. Box 489
Locust Valley, NY 11560　　　　Tel. (516) 676-1802

Incest Survivors
P.O. Box 5613
Long Beach, CA 90800

Johnson Institute
7151 Metro Boulevard
Minneapolis, MN 55435　　　　　Tel. (612) 944-0511

MIBCA: Minnesota Institute on Black Chemical Abuse
2616 Nicollet Avenue South
Minneapolis, MN 55408　　　　　Tel. (612) 871-7878

Multi-Cultural Prevention Work Group
Allegheny County MHMR/DA Program
429 Forbes Avenue, 9th Floor
Pittsburgh, PA 15219　　　　　　Tel. (412) 355-4291

NAATP: National Association of Addiction Treatment
    Programs, Inc.
2082 Michelson Drive, Suite 304
Irvine, CA 92715   Tel. (714) 476-8204

NACOA: National Association for Children of Alcoholics, Inc.
31706 Coast Highway, Suite 201
South Laguna, CA 92677-3044   Tel. (714) 499-3889

NADAC: National Association of Alcoholism and Drug
    Abuse Counselors, Inc.
3717 Columbia Pike, Suite 300
Arlington, VA 22204   Tel. (703) 920-4644

NALGAP: National Association of Lesbian and Gay
    Alcoholism Professionals, Inc.
204 West 20th Street
New York, NY 10011   Tel. (212) 807-0634

Narcotics Anonymous
World Services Office, Inc.
P.O. Box 9999
Van Nuys, CA 91409   Tel. (818) 780-3951

NASADAD: National Association of State Alcohol and Drug
    Abuse Directors, Inc.
44 North Capitol. Street, N.W., Suite 520
Washington DC 20001   Tel. (202) 783-6868

NBAC: National Black Alcoholism Council
417 South Dearborn, Suite 700
Chicago, IL 60605   Tel. (312) 341-9466

NCA: National Council on Alcoholism, Inc.
12 West 21st Street, 7th Floor
New York, NY 10010   Tel. (212) 206-6770

NCADI: National Clearinghouse for Alcohol and Drug
    Information
1776 East Jefferson Street
Rockville, MD 20852   Tel. (301) 468-2600

NCCA: National Clergy Council on Alcoholism
1200 Varnum Street, N.E.
Washington, DC 20017   Tel. (202) 832-381

National Association for Children of Alcoholics
31582 Coast Highway, Suite B
South Laguna, CA 92677   Tel. (714) 499-3889

National Coalition for the Prevention of Drug and Alcohol Abuse
Quest International
6655 Sharon Woods Boulevard
Columbus, OH 43229 Tel. (614) 882-6400

National Coalition of Hispanic Health and Human Services Organizations
1030-15th Street, N.W., Suite 1053
Washington, DC 20005 Tel. (202) 371-2100

NIAAA: National Institute on Alcohol Abuse and Alcoholism
Parklawn Building, Room 16-105
5600 Fishers Lane
Rockville, MD 20857 Tel. (301) 443-388

NIDA: National Institute on Drug Abuse
Parklawn Building, Room 10-05
5600 Fishers Lane
Rockville, MD 20857 Tel. (301) 443-4577

National Prevention Network
c/o NASADAD
444 North Capitol Street, N.W., Suite 520
Washington, DC 20001 Tel. (202) 783-6868

NNSA: National Nurses Society on Addiction
2506 Gross Point Road
Evanston, IL 60201 Tel. (312) 475-7300

Overeaters Anonymous
World Service Office
2190 90th Street
Torrance, CA 90504 Tel. (213) 542-8263

Rutgers University Center of Alcohol Studies Library
P.O. Box 969
Piscataway, N.J. 08854 Tel. (201) 932-4442

Women for Sobriety, Inc.
P.O. Box 618
Quackertown, PA 18951 Tel. (215) 536-8026

Hunter House
SELF-HELP AND RECOVERY FOR ADULTS AND TEENS

SEXUAL HEALING: A Self-Help Program to Enhance Your Sensuality by Barbara Keesling, Ph.D.

A program to enhance sensuality and increase sexual confidence. All exercises are explained in detail. The author, a practicing surrogate partner and licensed psychologist, is uniquely qualified to present this powerful system of sensate focus exercises.

288 pages ... paperback ... $12.95

TURNING YOURSELF AROUND: Self-Help Strategies for Troubled Teens Kendall Johnson, Ph.D.

This is a support book for young adults, ages 15–20, who are going through 12-step programs. It follows the stories of three young people. The book provides overviews of the issues, followed by provocative questions and exercises that will help all teens deal with life issues. A pullout guide for parents, teachers, or counselors is included.

224 pages ... paperback ... $9.95

WHEN SOMEONE YOU LOVE IS IN THERAPY
by Michael Gold, Ph.D., with Marie Scampini

Explains the ins and outs of therapy to those whose loved ones are going through it, and answers such questions as "Why did they go into therapy?" "What do they do there?", "How do I know if something goes wrong?" and "What about me?"

256 pages ... paperback ... $10.95 ... available February 1993

WRITING FROM WITHIN: A Unique Guide to Writing Your Life's Stories by Bernard Selling

Any writer can create vivid autobiographical stories and life narratives using the techniques taught in this book—and in Selling's widely followed classes and workshops. Also used in 12-Step programs for working through the 4th step—taking a life inventory.

288 pages ... paperback ... 2nd edition ... $11.95

SAFE DIETING FOR TEENS by Linda Ojeda, Ph.D.

A program of exercise and calorie counting that will help teens take unwanted pounds off and keep them off. Ojeda encourages healthier, balanced eating habits, and gives teens a lot of personal options and choices, allowing them to design their own diets.

128 pages ... paperback ... $7.95

**Prices subject to change without notice
See over for ordering and discounts**

ORDER FORM

10% DISCOUNT on orders of $20 or more —
20% DISCOUNT on orders of $50 or more —
30% DISCOUNT on orders of $250 or more —
On cost of books for fully prepaid orders

NAME

ADDRESS

CITY/STATE   ZIP

COUNTRY (outside USA)   POSTAL CODE

TITLE	QTY	PRICE	TOTAL
Reclaiming Your Future		@ $ 10.95	
Safe Dieting For Teens		@ $ 7.95	
Sexual Healing		@ $ 12.95	
Trauma in the Lives . . . *(paperback)*		@ $ 15.95	
Trauma in the Lives . . . *(hardcover)*		@ $ 24.95	
When Someone You Love Is in Therapy		@ $ 10.95	
Writing from Within		@ $ 11.95	

Shipping costs:
First book: $2.00 ($3.00 for Canada)
Each additional book: $.50 ($1.00 for Canada)
For UPS rates and bulk orders call us at (510) 865-5282

TOTAL _____
Less discount @ _____ %   (_____)
TOTAL COST OF BOOKS _____
Calif. residents add sales tax _____
Shipping & handling _____
TOTAL ENCLOSED _____
Please pay in U.S. funds only

❏ Check   ❏ Money Order   ❏ Visa   ❏ M/C

Card # _____ Exp date _____

Signature _____

Complete and mail to:

Hunter House Inc., Publishers
PO Box 2914, Alameda CA 94501-2914
Phone (510) 865-5282 Fax (510) 865-4295

❏ Check here to receive our book catalog